IBM

THE MAKING
OF THE
COMMON VIEW

IBM

THE MAKING
OF THE
COMMON VIEW

Michael Killen

HARCOURT BRACE JOVANOVICH, PUBLISHERS
Boston   San Diego   New York

Requests for permission to make copies of any part of the work
should be mailed to:
Permissions, Harcourt Brace Jovanovich, Publishers,
Orlando, Florida 32887

The following publishers have given permission to use
quotations from copyrighted works:
The definition of distributed data processing from
Dictionary of Computing, copyright 1987 by
International Business Machines Corporation.
The definition of an applications program from
The Dictionary of Computing,
copyright 1983 by Oxford University Press.
March 17, 1987 Programming Announcement
"Systems Application Architecture"
reprinted by permission of
International Business Machines Corporation.

Printed in the United States of America

Library of Congress Cataloging-in-Publication Data

Killen, Michael.
IBM-- the making of the common view.
1. International Business Machines Corporation.
2. Computer industry. I. Title
HD9696.C64I48475 1988   338.7′61004′0973   88-2189
ISBN 0—15—143480—8

First edition
A B C D E

To my loving wife Josephine
and the kids,
Michael David (Max),
Karl,
and Diana.

Contents

Author's Note

Researching this book was a challenge. However, I had several things going for me. First, I knew where a good number of the IBM "wild ducks" nested. They pointed me to other IBM wild ducks who would bend IBM rules and talk fairly openly to me. Second, long before IBM discovered that a fledgling Bob Woodward was in its midst, 80% of the research had already been completed. By then it did not matter too much if most of the wild ducks headed for cover.

A quote from Lenin, "He who wins out has the best people, organization, and machines," helps to explain the third thing going for me. For machines, I had two networked high-performance workstations with six and four megabytes of main memory and a total of 330 megabytes of on-line disk storage, and an Imagen laser printer with five megabytes of main memory and a twenty megabyte hard disk. For software, I used Frame Maker™'s text processing package. Basically, I had the equivalent of two Mack trucks that handled like BMWs.

For people, I had even more horsepower. Edie Gaert-
ner tirelessly helped to pull this manuscript together.
You only begin to appreciate Edie's contribution when
you learn that I spell phonetically, at my best, and I
have never learned, so could not forget, rules of grammar. Even with the aid of several MIPs of computer
power, she had a task most editors would have crum-
bled under. Organization and production were left to
Edie, too.

Finally, I would like to acknowledge everyone who
contributed to this undertaking, however small or large
the contribution.

Preface

Sometime in 1983 I was eating dinner at a local Palo Alto, California, restaurant that might have been frequented by many of the characters in Tom Wolfe's Electric Kool-Aid Gang, when my lunch partner—a white-shirted, pin-stripe-suited IBMer—said something about IBM that piqued my attention. It would take more than three years before I would say, "Of course! That's what he was talking about." An IBM announcement released on March 17, 1987, triggered my memory of that luncheon and the importance of what he had said.

We had finished talking about my work on the various issues facing the computer industry at the time. Between forkfuls of spaghetti and sips of wine, the discussion drifted to my acquaintance's work at IBM.

He said something that sounded strange—IBM was setting up four "colored" teams. I was sure he said "colored." But it didn't make sense that IBM would set up teams of black employees. IBM had no Equal Employment Opportunity ruling against it that I knew of to warrant setting up teams of black employees. Besides, I had thought that practice was illegal, and by 1983, most people no longer referred to Negroes as "coloreds" but as blacks. It didn't make sense that IBM was setting up "color" teams either.

Not to sound foolish I asked, "It's a little unusual for you folks to form teams based on color, isn't it?" The question was framed to provide an opportunity for him to explain. What he said next also surprised me.

"You're right, we've never done it before. It's new to a lot of us." Then he shoveled another forkful of spaghetti into his mouth. A few chews and a swallow later he continued: "I guess the reason we are doing it is because the development of computer products has become so complicated that we had to try another approach." I nodded. He went on to say that in his twenty-odd years in IBM development jobs, he couldn't remember another time when IBM had taken that approach.

I decided to hazard a question: "What are those teams supposed to do?"

He looked up, paused, and said, "I'm not sure I can tell you. That might be confidential information." At that point I would have dropped my fork; however, I didn't want to accentuate what he said.

"God!" I said to myself, "How many years have I been talking to executives from IBM, AT&T, DEC, and other companies? Maybe ten. I should have known better than to phrase a question in such a way that it would make my lunch partner uncomfortable." Obtaining so-called "confidential" information has never been my goal. Because the computer industry is so complex, it is a big enough job just making sense out of visible actions without having to determine what the so-called "confidential" information means. And I shouldn't have asked a question that would impede communication.

IBM, Apple, AT&T, DEC, H-P, Bell South, US West, and other mammoth computer and communication companies around the world have my name in their data bases. They categorize me as an industry analyst, a consultant, the press, or a market research analyst —someone who produces several major studies each year that explain the strategies of the very large computer and communication companies and that explain the impact and opportunities the execution of those strategies will create for others. When these companies announce a new product or make pricing, financial, or other organizational changes, I usually receive a copy of the announcement. (Maybe they think I don't read the newspapers and magazines?) Because I read their announcements, *The Wall Street Journal*, and the industry's trade press, the odds are that if IBM had formed either colored or color teams, I would know that. The entire industry would know it.

After clearing his thoughts and throat, my IBMer companion said he thought it would be okay to tell me about the teams. However, he wanted me to agree never to attribute this bit of trivia to him—it could, at the least, cause him some embarrassment.

I assured him: "You need never be concerned that I would ever link this to you."

He continued without divulging any confidential information: "We set up four colored teams to help manage 370 software development."

Amazed, I said, "You did?"

"Yeah, we've got a Green, Red, Blue, and Yellow Team. Four colored teams." At that point I chuckled to myself and said, "What, no black team?" Then he looked surprised.

"No. No black team. Just the four colors I mentioned. Don't know why we picked those colors. But we did not use black."

At that point, I realized that all along the man sitting across from me had been saying color teams. The joke was on me. I felt amused, perhaps a little foolish, but certainly relieved.

But one bit of information he had revealed really intrigued me. It was not that teams were "helping to manage 370 software." That's too general a statement to have much significance. Hundreds, perhaps thousands of IBMers work on 370 software. For years they have been doing that. No, it was something else—the *number* of the teams. The number four intrigued me. Why four teams; why not three or five? Why did they need four teams to do something? Couldn't IBM get the job done with one team like the rest of us?

I asked my associate: "Why four teams?" Nonchalantly, he replied: "Because there are four problems, one team for each problem." He paused, so I tried to prime him. "Four problems?" It didn't work. He laughed and said, "I can't [won't] tell you the four problems. Besides I don't completely understand the big picture."

I respected his need for nondisclosure and switched the conversation to a different topic. However, for the next week or two, I occasionally reflected on that luncheon, particularly on his revelation that there were four teams and four problems. What set of four problems had IBM identified? For what four problems had

IBM mobilized four teams, each named by a color? Although I could list many problems IBM faced, I could not determine which four problems it had identified in this case. After several weeks passed, I forgot about the subject until late March 1987.

A few days after March 17, I sorted through my mail and discovered the "ivories." Ivories is computer industry talk for IBM's product and pricing announcements, which are printed on white or ivory-colored paper. This ivory was unusual. It didn't announce a series of new products or any product as best I could tell. Ivories don't usually announce IBM financial information. Nor do they iterate organizational changes. Rather, this five-page, tightly written, highly exact ivory heralded a change of direction. That's all.

That's all! That near-cryptic ivory that I held in my hand meant that IBM—the elephantine company of the computer industry—had decided to make a left turn. The announcement, in very exact terminology, alerted all who might now be in its path and all who wanted to travel with it exactly where it was going.

For those who missed that announcement, you will begin to appreciate the magnitude of it when you read the following excerpt from David E. Sanger's *New York Times'* article "IBM's Moment of Truth," published nine months after the announcement. Referring to the announcement, Sanger wrote: "The solution everyone is waiting for, in fact, is a product that will never be sold separately and almost defies explanation."

For our purposes we can focus on the words "almost defies explanation." When the *New York Times*, winner of 58 Pulitzer Prizes, writes that something "almost defies explanation," I get the message. It's big, and it's complex. For that reason, I won't attempt to explain it here.

In that same Sunday, January 3, 1988 article, Sanger quoted Apple Computer's John Sculley, who in reference to IBM's March 17, 1987 announcement said: "It is far too little, far too late." I won't comment on Sculley's statement here, except to note that the announcement was obviously important enough for him to try to diminish it.

When I first read the announcement, I sensed its importance. I can't explain why I felt that way. I certainly did not by any means comprehend all that I was reading. I think everyone has had a similar experience —they have come upon something they did not understand, but for various reasons (not necessarily conscious), they recognized its importance. That's what happened to me.

I could tell on some level that the scope and breadth of the announcement were enormous. Users of IBM's personal computers, midrange, and mainframe computers would be impacted by that announcement. The same was true for management information systems (MIS) people, their systems analysts and programming staffs; the thousands of software companies; and all of IBM's competitors.

After re-reading the announcement several times, I still struggled with its contents. After having analyzed so many IBM announcements and written so many studies describing IBM's strategies, I could not understand why I was having such a difficult time absorbing the context of what was announced and its impact.

I began to study IBM's presentation of the information. I counted the number of "concepts" that the announcement addressed. One set that seemed to cut across every other issue came to four. That's right, four. But I still had not connected that to what I had heard in that Palo Alto restaurant back in 1983. I first had to say to myself that it would be a lot easier for me and everyone else if IBM presented what it wanted to present using fewer concepts. Humans think well about one, two, or three concepts at a time. Beyond three, thinking becomes more difficult. That was why I had a problem comprehending the information—too many concepts.

IBM's announcement seemed to require four concepts. Once I realized that, the number four hurled me back to the restaurant at the base of the Cardinal hotel and my luncheon with my friend from IBM. From deep in my memory came the words *colored, color,* and *four.* That's right—four teams and four problems. At that moment I was certain that a relationship existed between the four concepts or elements of computing addressed in the March 17 announcement and the four teams, each named by a color and each attacking one of four problems.

When I made that connection, it was like a blast of fresh air blowing away the cobwebs in my mind. I could trace the roots of that March 17, 1987 announcement back to early 1983. It helped justify my sense that this was an important announcement—four teams attacking four problems for more than three years.

Weeks later, maybe a month later, it became clear to me that the announcement heralded the beginning of the most sweeping change of direction IBM had made in more than a decade (maybe much longer). This might be the spark that could ignite a renaissance of the slightly lethargic giant. I knew that the face of the computer industry would change and that great numbers of people would be affected. Possibly, IBM was launching a brave new strategy that future computer historians would cite as the beginning of a new era.

Still not fully comprehending all the ramifications of the announcement—I suspect no one will know the full impact of this announcement for 25 years, if ever —I made two decisions.

The first: this announcement was so important that before March ended I would begin a study analyzing the strategy and speculating on its impact and opportunities for others. I knew that MIS directors, heads of software companies, the large consulting companies, other computer vendors, and some IBMers would want an outside opinion of just what it was that "almost defies explanation." That study became available to the industry in July 1987.

The second decision grew out of the first: I believed that a lot of people would be interested in the story of how IBM engineered what it said it would do. The result is this book—*IBM: The Making Of The Common View*—the behind-the-scenes story of the people and events that led to the March 17 announcement.

All the people in this book are real people except for the Armonk Administrative Assistant, the two young IBMers in the Montvale cafeteria, and Carl Crawford. They are fictional characters created as vehicles for presenting concepts and for moving the story line. However, while fictional, the actions of these characters are quite real. I have known Administrative Assistants like the one presented here.

Carl is a composite of many IBMers I have met over the years, especially those "wild ducks" who have helped me navigate through the back channels of IBM to find information I have needed.

I believe that the events described in this book represent an accurate accounting of what actually took place during the years preceding the March 17 announcement. The IBM executives who took part, the dates, the technology issues, the locations, even the storm that hit Raleigh, North Carolina, are factual.

The reader needs to know, however, that I clearly invited myself into the minds of the main characters. The thoughts presented are my thoughts about what they may have been thinking. However, great pain has been taken to depict some semblance of what was going on in their heads. In doing so, I may have made mistakes—the topic is complex and so are the people. To any whom I may have incorrectly characterized, I sincerely apologize. But until Earl Wheeler—the central figure in this book and the IBM executive who had the brilliance and courage to attempt to do what he and others did—tells his story, this book, imperfect as it may be, remains the only source of what happened behind the thick walls of IBM.

The writer's intent in this undertaking has never been a witch hunt. Rather, the intent has been to tell an important story about the people in IBM who attempted to do something significant. It is an attempt to understand what happened and to tell the story as accurately as I could, as a "quasi" insider, and as objectively as I could, as an outsider.

Although I may have failed in areas to reach this goal, my aim is to enable the reader to discover some interesting, even valuable, insights into the computer industry and its technology. I hope that all who read this book will find in it a valuable experience. Perhaps readers will begin to understand what almost defies explanation and to create their own perceptions of the Common View.

Michael Killen
Palo Alto, California

1   Armonk, New York

FEBRUARY 18, 1987

A few miles north of White Plains, New York, Route 22 passes the Kensico Reservoir. Up the road and to the right, a sign announces the entrance to Old Orchard Road, a private road cut into a hillside. Old Orchard rises, turns right, and then curves gently to the left past a white security station a hundred yards up the hill. Only invited guests or drivers wearing valid identification badges may pass this point.

No more than 20 yards farther up Old Orchard Road, a parking lot dotted with bare trees appears on the driver's left. Beyond the parking area, a long, white, three-story building sits atop the gentle slope of a hill. At its front, an odd structure protrudes perpendicularly from the center.

On this cold, cloudy, February morning, a dark Detroit–made car turned on to Old Orchard Road, passed the security station, and paused in front of the

1

building. John Akers, Chairman of IBM, emerged from the back seat, closed the top of his overcoat, and quickly disappeared into the IBM World Headquarters.

Later this same morning, six top-level IBM executives parked their cars in unmarked spaces, an IBM custom, and walked into the building. These executives rank among the most powerful group of computer people in the world and form the most powerful group of executives in IBM. They are members of the IBM Management Committee (MC).

John Akers and the MC came to Armonk for meetings that would last throughout the day. The Management Committee Conference Room, IBM's most sacred meeting place, reflects a sedate quality with its yellow rug, off-white ceiling, wood-paneled cabinets and lectern, and the large, arc-shaped conference tables resting on gleaming chrome bases. The watchful eye of Thomas Watson stares out from a large oil painting centered on the back wall.

Just as Camelot had King Arthur, its knights, and its round table; IBM has Akers, its Management Committee, and the crescent–shaped tables.

Shortly before the morning meeting convened, the committee members took their regular places. Akers quickly walked into the room and took the chair at the center of the front table. IBM protocol dictates that whenever the Chairman visits any IBM facility, he sit at the center of the table.

Since the table arcs forward, by leaning slightly forward and looking to his right or left, Akers can easily see the other members of the MC. Today, those members included Paul Rizzo, Allen Krowe, Jack Kuehler,

Clarence (Jack) Rogers, Kaspar V. Cassani, and Frank Metz. Each runs an IBM corporate staff department or a major line organization.

As the attendees removed papers from their briefcases and readied themselves for the business at hand, someone joked: "Look at the scratches and dents on this table. Business is not so bad that we can't get the tops of these tables refinished once in a while." It was true that IBM's earnings had not grown at the usual 15% per year that everyone had come to expect. In the spirit of the moment, another attendee retorted, "That table looks like that because you drop your briefcase on it every time you sit down. If you did that at home, your wife would throw you out."

A third executive, looking at his own table which had its share of scratches, joined the discussion: "Hey, it's got to be the members of the Board of Directors who mess these up. Maybe we should stop letting them use this room!" "It wouldn't help our image if the public knew we didn't keep our desks *looking crisp*," chimed in another member. General laughter filled the room.

By now, nearly everyone had examined the state of the table tops and found them less than praiseworthy, but no one could say that about the men in the first row. Each man is impeccably dressed, and each has exceptional ability. Any one of them could make a good IBM chairman. One or two would make an outstanding chairman. Together they possess a tremendous amount of knowledge about people, computers, technology, and markets. Each man knows where IBM has been and where it needs to go. Today they will tap that knowledge to make an important decision. Their decision

will be based, at least in part, on their experience of the
events surrounding the development of System/360,
which was introduced in 1964.

Development of the System/360

The mission of the System 360's developers was to create a single, compatible product line of computers that
had common software. With that in mind, management stipulated specifications that adhered to the strategic intent of the 360 project: individual models should
be suitable for both *scientific* and *commercial* batch work;
there should be a common operating system—OS/360;
there would (eventually) be a single programming language—PL/1. ISAM (Index Sequential Access Method)
was all that would be necessary for accessing and orga-
nizing data.

Management knew it could save millions of dollars
in development, manufacturing, and support costs by
producing a single, compatible line rather than coming
out with incompatible products. Engineers familiar
with the circuitry of one model, for example, could easily apply that knowledge to other models. Procedures
and equipment put in place to assemble and test one
model could easily be replicated or modified slightly to
produce the other models. Best of all, fewer programmers would be needed: only one group of programmers
would be needed for each of the three software functions—operating system, access/data management, and
PL/1 language development. This approach clearly min-
imized costs.

It also helped to limit the scope of the project. No company had ever attempted to develop a system as ambitious as the 360. The requirement of making software compatible across the product line excluded many options that would otherwise have increased the project's complexity.

The mission to create a single, compatible product line of computers with common software also held an important marketing promise. When a customer's application(s) outgrew a Model 30 (because of the need for additional processing power or memory), a Model 40 could be installed, then a Model 50, and then a Model 65. Because of hardware/software compatibility, the

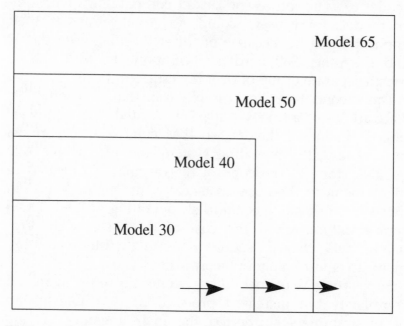

Figure 1 - Orderly Applications Growth on the IBM System/360

same applications could be run, and there would be minimal impact on the end user. This permitted *orderly* growth of user applications up the product line (Figure 1) and enabled the marketing people to fulfill a marketer's dream—to attract new customers and to keep the old.

A Break with the Plan

But in the 1960s, IBM's management started to diverge from its original 360 mission. The tenet of a single hardware design collapsed when the company built the Model 67. This processor lacked compatibility with other models, and users could not easily transfer their applications to it. Because of differences between the 67 and the other 360 hardware components, IBM had to train a separate group of people to support the 67.

The second tenet to crumble was that of compatible software. An attractive market existed for a lower-priced version of the 360, so IBM created a new model by rewriting the operating system and placing its code on disk storage. The code of the original 360 resided in main memory. Because costs for main memory exceed those for disk storage, the disk operating system (DOS) significantly lowered the cost of the system. Unfortunately, this created a dual operating system environment, an environment of incompatibility.

Supporting two operating systems not only increased complexity but increased production costs. One group of programmers supported the main memory version of the operating system (OS), another supported the

DOS version. One group of programmers now had to support ISAM on the main memory version, a second supported it on DOS. The same applied to PL/1. The addition of another operating system that was not compatible with all the models weakened the strategic intent of compatible software at its base.

At the same time, M.I.T., Bell Labs, and a few other important IBM accounts chose to install GE computers. Large users of computers were attracted to GE because it had a time share, interactive operating system. IBM's OS/360 had been designed to provide batch services; providing service to terminal users had been an afterthought. To meet the threat posed by GE and to seize the opportunity of the emerging interactive business, IBM introduced its Time Sharing System—TSS. IBM now had three operating systems running on 360 hardware.

Besides abandoning the tenet of a single compatible family of software, IBM strayed off course in other areas. Users wanted to access their computer systems via terminals; ISAM did not have what it takes to effectively access data and application programs. Users wanted to develop applications more effectively; ISAM did not have what it takes to manage data effectively. So IBM offered various combinations of access methods and data base management systems: an early version of Information Management System (IMS), General Information Systems (GIS), and Customer Information Control System (CICS). IBM added more variables by offering additional programming languages as well. Besides PL/1, the language IBM wanted everyone to write programs in, IBM added support for COBOL and FORTRAN. Compatibility of access methods and of the data base and programming languages had been compromised.

Within a few years of the introduction of the System/360, IBM executives had veered significantly from the fundamental product development mission for that product. In retrospect, however, the fact remains that after overwhelming problems with the scheduling of hardware delivery and the availability of systems software, the System/360 turned out to be the most significant technological and marketing achievement the computer industry had ever seen. IBM's success with the 360 catapulted the company to leadership of the world computer market.

This raises a question: How could IBM or anyone veer so far from its original mission and still succeed so spectacularly? The answer lies partly in recognizing that a mission statement describes just an ideal. One can strive for the ideal and possibly obtain it in an ideal world, but the early planners of the 360 worked in a world of compromises and tradeoffs. They gave up pursuit of the ideal to seize the opportunity to sell more computers now. Fortunately for IBM, it had traveled far enough on course so that when it veered away, much of the foundation for long-term success had already been laid.

The Lessons Learned

What did the executives sitting in the first row of the MC Conference Room learn from the 360 experience? How does that experience affect their thinking today?

They may think that an *ideal* mission for any company in the computer business is to field a single family of computers with compatible software. But these men also know that is not practical for a company like IBM. IBM provides computers to so many different clients with such diverse requirements that no single family of computers could begin to meet the objectives.

Although a single family of hardware is not practical, these executives will probably always strive for software compatibility within a computer family. This strategy has been exceptionally successful in promoting growth in the installed hardware base, and the growth has been largely achieved without substantive changes in the applications themselves, but rather through changes in the operating environments of those applications.

The experience probably also taught them never to back a project with risks comparable to those of the 360. The 360 project turned out to be a *bet your company* undertaking. In all fairness, any organization other than IBM would probably have been destroyed by the technological complexity and multiplicity of problems that followed the System/360 announcement. The achievement stands as a tribute to the single-minded dedication of the IBM organization and to its financial and human resources.

The executives present in the MC Conference Room today reflect this rich historical perspective. In addition, they manage vast financial and human resources. It is well that they do because today IBM is called upon to face a greater problem of incompatibility than it ever faced with the 360 family. It now has three incompatible families—the personal computer, the midrange or 3X family, and the 370 family. These gentlemen will be asked to call upon their collective resources to solve this dilemma.

———————

The lights suddenly dim in the MC Conference Room. A staff member has turned down the wall rheostat a quarter of a turn. Someone is heard to ask Jack Kuehler, "How did it go yesterday?"

Kuehler had held a press conference the day before at which IBM announced the incorporation of the new one megabyte memory chip in some of its low-end systems. The advanced chip would be used in the 1986-announced RT version of the Personal Computer and in a new PC that would be announced within two weeks.

Kuehler never had a chance to respond to the question. The door closed, and the meeting began. He and the others would now focus on the serious business of running IBM.

2   Montvale, New Jersey

FEBRUARY 18, 1987—EARLY MORNING

The Hudson River separates the eastern border of New Jersey from lower New York State. New York's Rockland County sits to the north. These two boundaries plus a ragged vertical line drawn southeasterly from the Ramapo River to the Passaic River and south to Route 108 enclose a dozen or so medium-sized cities and several hundred townships. They collectively comprise the county of Bergen.

A string of Bergen County towns—Mahwah, Upper Saddle River, Old Tappan, and Montvale—dot the New Jersey border. In the border town of Montvale early this cold Wednesday morning, two young IBM employees huddled in the company's cafeteria. Both had just come in from the chilly February air.

Between bites of a doughnut, the young man was saying with conviction: "I wish I could have gone to headquarters with him today. It would have been the chance of a lifetime."

The young woman sitting across from him had no idea who her friend and colleague was referring to, but she knew he would soon tell her.

On at least two previous occasions he had given her some tips on how to rise in the IBM organization. Actually, his approach didn't appeal to her; it frightened her. The young programmer had pointed out, "If you want a shot at the fast track here, you have to get discovered. You have to do it in a big way, and it has to happen early in your career, definitely by the time you hit 25."

He had further divulged that he would do almost anything to be discovered by the IBM Management Committee. He believed that if they knew he existed and if they liked the way he handled himself, which he knew they would, someone on that committee would tap him for a promotion. They would move him to a more challenging position in another division or in one of the corporate staff departments. There he would work hard and keep himself in front of the MC members. If he landed an assignment in one of the divisions, he'd then position himself to seize a good staff assignment. If he had a staff assignment, he'd then arrange to get back into one of the divisions, especially a fast-growing department. Like someone in a sailboat tacking back and forth across a body of water, but never going backwards more than a few feet, he planned to change direction continually until he reached his destination. Once near the top, he figured he would have the right mix of experience to qualify him as a candidate for the Chairman's position.

The young woman chuckled to herself as she recalled his answer to why discovery by the age of 25 was so critical. With a straight face he had responded, "Once you get on the fast track you need to stay on that roller coaster for another 25 years. It takes that long to accumulate what you need to run this company. If you don't get going at 25, you won't arrive in time. You have to get there by 50 or else you lose your edge over everyone else." He had flashed a full set of white teeth as he said emphatically, "Actually, we call it the Akers Edge."

He had known that she would ask him what that meant, and when she did, he explained, "When you arrive at the top, you need an edge. You want to do it the way Akers did it. When John Opel (IBM Chairman before Akers) retired, most of the candidates had already hit their mid-fifties. Take Paul Rizzo, for example. I think he had 55 years under his belt when they looked for the next chairman. Anyone in their mid-fifties could only run the company for another few years."

"Remember," he had continued, "tradition in IBM is that the Chairman retires at 60. Akers, at 50, has an edge. He holds the promise of a decade of uninterrupted leadership, and that's an important advantage. None of the others could promise that and still retire at 60."

Coming back to the reality of the cafeteria, she asked: "Who is going up to headquarters today?"

"Hanrahan," he answered.

Dick Hanrahan was Vice President of Programming at the headquarters of IBM's Entry Systems Division, or ESD, as IBMers refer to it where both young people worked.

Like most employees, she found the actions of the high and mighty interesting, but to her ambitious young colleague, they were fascinating.

Don Estridge, who founded ESD in 1981, led IBM's initial charge into the personal computer market. The force and momentum of Estridge's drive enabled IBM to capture the lion's share of the PC market, a market that thousands of software and hardware companies could enter. In 1984 Estridge transferred to IBM's Corporate Manufacturing Department. Shortly thereafter he and his wife, along with several other IBM employees and fellow travelers, lost their lives in a Delta Airline plane crash at Dallas-Fort Worth Airport.

About a year before Estridge's death, Bill Lowe emerged as the division's second president. Much as the Marines get all the credit for storming the beaches and leading the charge, and the Army is thought to follow them and mop up, Lowe has walked in the shadows of Estridge's success. Like most people, the two young IBM employees thought Lowe had merely "maintained" ESD since Estridge's reign. That, however, is not the case. Lowe has been given a special objective. If he accomplishes that mission, he will make as much or more of a contribution to IBM's success than Estridge made. As Lowe's Vice President of Programming, Hanrahan plays a key part in this plan. Neither of the two persons at the table knew this.

"So what makes you think that Dick is going to present to the MC today?" the young woman asked her programmer friend. Before he could respond, she continued, "I bet it's to fix the date for the PS/2 announcement."

Looking surprised and shocked, he proclaimed: "Wrong, wrong, wrong." His head shook back and forth like the pendulum of a clock. "How long have I been teaching you the ropes around here? How in the world did you ever come up with that idea?"

"First," she informed him, "I read somewhere that it now takes a company like IBM a little over two years to design a computer product of the PS/2's magnitude. It's common knowledge around the Montvale offices that IBM started work on the PS/2 back in early 1985 or late 1984. That means over two years have passed."

"Second," and this reason surprised him, "I was talking with a couple of programmers a few months ago who were visiting us from Austin, Texas."

"What group? The Data Manager group?" he interrupted. Using the product name, he was name-dropping a bit, but he needed to impress her with his knowledge.

She said, "I guess so, I'm not really familiar with the different groups over there. They're working on the data base management system for the OS/2."

He, like practically anyone else in ESD's executive offices or in the programming groups, knew that OS/2 was the operating system that accompanied IBM's new PS/2 product. It was not as well known within ESD that the Data Manager had been assigned to Austin.

"Yeah, Austin got the assignment to develop the Data Manager," he said, "but I'm not sure I understand why."

She interrupted his train of thought by questioning, "I know the Data Manager is a data base management program. Is it similar to dBASE III Plus® from Ashton-Tate?"

"Yes, the Data Manager fills the need for a DBMS (data base management system) for the PS/2. When we get it on the market, software companies that make DBMSs for the IBM personal computer market will have a rough time selling their product any more."

Then he said, "So why do you think Austin got the assignment for the Data Manager?" Not waiting for her reply or expecting that she would know, he went on, "I think its because they have a lot of programmers there who are familiar with small systems. They used to work on office automation products including the 5120, the 5520 and the Display Writer. They have an affinity for small machines."

Although the young woman's job in a plans and controls department that managed marketing expenses provided no information about that question, she guessed, "Maybe most of IBM's programmers with data base management experience work in Austin, too."

"No, we keep the real long-hairs out in San Jose," he laughed.

"That rings a bell," she said. "When I talked to the programmers from Austin, one of them mentioned that San Jose had loaned her to Austin. She came from a group in San Jose that supported the, let me think. . . that's it, the DB2."

"Sure, the DB2. It's another data base management system like the Data Manager, but it runs on big machines. What else did they tell you?"

"Not much except that some of the programmers from the DB2 team had completed their work and everyone planned to head back home. One of them said that he felt they were successful in making sure that Austin people understood what had to be done."

"Yeah, interfacing the Data Manager with DB2 is a big issue—and a big problem if it doesn't work."

"That's the other reason I thought that Hanrahan and the MC might decide to announce the PS/2," she commented. "The Californians going home might mean the issues are pretty well resolved. Maybe they are ready to announce. Oh, and I almost forgot." A smile lit her face. "A few weeks ago I saw a group of people with cameras, lights, reflectors, all sorts of photographic equipment, going into the upstairs conference room. When I elbowed my way into the room, there was a PS/2 on a white blanket. That's what they were photographing.

"So when I put two and two together, that seems to add up to the PS/2 announcement. What do you think?"

"Not bad, not bad at all. Actually, that is a pretty good deduction. However, the MC decided a few weeks ago to announce the PS/2, and they chose April 2. They wanted to do it earlier, but the earliest date available was April 1. The MC didn't want to risk a new product announcement on April Fool's day, so they settled for April 2."

"Then what's Hanrahan going up to the MC meeting for?"

A bit embarrassed by his lack of knowledge, he regretfully replied, "I don't know."

Then she asked, "How did you know in the first place that he had to be there today?"

"A week ago I tried to make an appointment to see him. I wanted to talk to him about the problem we have using the IBM AT and the 3270 terminals. You know, you use the AT for a few days and get used to the

layout of the keyboard and screen prompts. Then you
use the 3270 terminal to run the same application, and
the keyboard and the prompts are so different that you
lose a lot of time getting restarted. It's not just my problem, hundreds of people use these workstations every
day. I wanted to talk to him about standardizing the keyboard and other interfaces."

"What does that have to do with him going up to
Armonk today?" she wanted to know.

"Nothing except when Hanrahan's secretary logged
on to PROFS and called up Hanrahan's calendar I saw it
listed. That's how I know."

At this point the young woman stretched restlessly. It
was time to get back to work. The two picked up their
empty cups and napkins.

As they walked out of the cafeteria she prompted,
"Well, did you ever have your meeting with Hanrahan?"

"No, I got on his calendar, but then I got bumped. His
secretary told me Hanrahan just couldn't meet with me
at this time."

"And he's probably with the MC now." she replied.
"Sorry you can't be there with him."

"Yeah, me too," he said. "But I don't think he's there
yet."

"Why not?" she asked, looking up at him as they
stopped to turn the corner.

"Well, according to his calendar, he had a morning
meeting in Purchase, New York, first."

He waved goodbye with a parting look at her questioning face, then turned and took the corridor to the
left.

3 Northwest Airlines

In early January, Carl Crawford had taken a call in his Rochester, Minnesota, office from an Administrative Assistant from Armonk. The AA had introduced himself, described an assignment that Armonk wanted Carl to undertake, and explained that Carl had six weeks to research the subject. The assignment seemed straightforward enough. The AA would provide ideas as well as contacts and Carl should call the AA any time he needed assistance. The presentation was scheduled for the morning of February 18.

Carl had asked the AA why the presentation was scheduled specifically for the morning of the 18th. The AA replied, "I can't tell you too much, but in the afternoon we have a big gig planned. I *can* tell you that some people around here think it's a good idea to bring your findings to the MC's attention before that meeting occurs."

"What's happening in the afternoon?" he had asked.

"Look," he answered, "no disrespect to you, but it just ain't Kosher to talk about what's going on around here right now." He applied emphasis to the words *ain't* and *Kosher*. "With all the pressure to move people out of IBM staff positions into the field, I don't want to give anyone, anywhere, reason for them to ship me off to some Siberia."

During the second half of 1986, momentum had been building within IBM to do just that. All IBM corporate and divisional headquarters had orders to move as many people as they could out of staff positions and into field positions in an effort to acquire new sales and to support existing customers more effectively. In early January 1987, many IBMers feared—in varying degrees —that their supervisors might present them with a list of field openings and ask them to make a choice.

The AA's demeanor was serious. "You have an important assignment. Remember my advice. Get over to those four sites I mentioned as soon as possible—touch base with them. You know who to look for."

"Yeah, I got it." Crawford looked down at the note-scribbled piece of paper on his desk and read off what he had just written: Hanrahan in Montvale, Saranga in Milford, Casey in Raleigh, and Taradalsky in San Jose. "I'll start contacting them the first thing in the morning to set up meetings with each of them or whoever they assign to represent them. We'll get the information, synthesize the results, and see you on the 18th."

"You got it."

As soon as Carl had hung up the phone, he reviewed the conversation and began to make notes. As he did so, questions formed in his mind: Why these four men to meet with and not four others? Out of nearly 400,000 employees why those specific four men? What's so special about them? What ties them together? What commonalities exist? What disparities?

One thing was apparent from the briefing: all four were Vice Presidents and powerful.

Carl Crawford had met an occasional IBM VP on previous assignments. He had been impressed by some of them. He couldn't vouch for their technical knowledge or skills; not all would win personality contests. But whether a VP of a division, a group, or a corporate department, most appeared to fit the category of "movers and shakers." Crawford did not personally know any of these four men.

As he had reflected on this group, he mentally noted another important disparity: none of them worked in the same organization. Hanrahan worked in the Entry Systems Division, Saranga in the Information Systems Business Unit, Casey in the Communications Products Division, and Taradalsky in the Santa Teresa Lab.

The AA had mentioned that each of them came from a programming background, although in a different division. What would someone in the Communications Products Division on the East Coast have to do with someone in the Santa Teresa Lab on the West Coast?

Though Carl Crawford was unaware of it, there was a commonality in the circumstances of the four men: they shared a common mission and all had been invited to the afternoon Management Committee meeting on February 18.

Six weeks later, as Crawford boarded Northwest Airlines flight from the Minneapolis–St. Paul Airport, the answers to all his previous questions were obvious. The questions in his mind today centered on the presentation he would deliver the next day. The exact approach he would take had not yet jelled in his mind.

"Come on Carl," he said to himself, "this plane will land soon and before you get off you'd better have your approach 100% nailed." Then an old, uncomfortable feeling came over him, one he had experienced many times in his life. It was the kind of feeling he had had as a kid when he had waited until the last minute to do his homework and then worried whether he had enough time left to pull it off.

Quickly opening his brief case, he removed his notes, some writing paper, and a manila folder containing a few dozen overhead transparencies. He paused for a moment, the light dawning in his eyes, as he realized that IBM had never before assigned him a task like this one. A smile came over his face as he thought about that.

Carl Crawford's assignment for the February 18 briefing was to present to the Management Committee the accurate and precise definitions of several key computer terms and concepts—definitions that would enable the executives to think clearly about crucial topics affecting IBM's future. These men had to gauge how business enterprises would configure their computer systems in the future. Would the enterprises invest in centralized computing? Dispersed data processing? Cooperative processing? Enterprise processing? How could they understand how these companies would move unless they had a complete picture of what the terms mean, knew the differences between them, and had a thorough grasp of the factors influencing a company to move in one direction rather than another. No one who runs a company like IBM, Hewlett-Packard, DEC, or Wang, or a software company, can do an adequate job without thoroughly understanding these terms.

Crawford had explained to his family that the people who run management information systems (MIS) in companies such as American Express, General Motors, Sears, and others use these terms all day long, but some of them, even those managing large systems of computers, have forgotten or lack a basic understanding of the concepts. It is easy to understand why, when you realize that technology and society are changing almost daily.

Crawford took a sip of the scotch he had ordered. Facing the challenge at hand, he tentatively began to sketch his opening remarks:

> Gentlemen. You are all, of course, aware that users of computers initially concentrated their computer power in one place. The computer(s), the operations staff, the programming organization, and the administrative function were all placed in one central location. We define that form of computing as *centralized* data processing.

He had introduced the first concept: centralized data processing.

Even though some of these men helped write the book on centralized data processing, Crawford thought that he should briefly state the primary applications that people run on their centralized systems. He decided he would now say:

> You all know that the central site processed
> the enterprise's *production* data processing
> applications and requirements.

If he used the word *enterprise*, he knew he would not
have to spell out business, governments, educational
institutions, etc. At the risk of boring them, he decided
he would proceed by stating that production data processing applications included the preparation of customer invoices and employee paychecks, the printing
of MIS reports, the *care and feeding* of the corporate data
bases, and the functioning of any other data processing
application directly related to running an enterprise.

Scribbling on his legal pad, he wrote:

> Possible objections to this definition.

It was possible that someone might think that that's
an antiquated way to think of the role of centralized systems and the computer resources that would be necessary to run tomorrow's enterprises. And he would
have a good point.

The role of the centralized computer, the host-based
system, had been changing primarily because the needs
to run an enterprise had been changing. Technological
advances in computers and communications fostered
those changes.

He decided he would say:

> Today we need to think of the centralized
> site in a new light. It is much more than just
> a processor of production data processing.
> Our customers will increasingly create net-
> works of computers throughout their enter-

prises. In fact, in the near future, they will become supremely dependent on them.

All these thoughts about the future were true, and Crawford took them seriously. He believed that everyone in a company would have workstations on their desks and that all workstations would be interconnected. People would become so dependent on the machines and the resources the network provided that it would no longer make sense for them to work without them.

At this point, he began to be inspired and excited by his own rhetoric. His sense of the dramatic began to take over.

> Gentlemen, the effective operation of a computer network will soon become a requirement for running all enterprises.
>
> If our customers fail to create networks or if the networks they do create do not work effectively, that enterprise will become uncompetitive in the very near future.

Then he thought he'd raise his voice a little and with great determination postulate:

> You all know that the new requirement of the centralized site must include the control and management of the enterprise's computer network.
>
> The centralized site must fill the need for controlling the enterprise's network. It must no longer be viewed as a central unconnect-

ed site. Rather, it must be viewed as an integral part of the network and the main control point of an enterprise's processing and
information system.

He took a deep breath. Thinking through each
thought and the words he planned to use excited him
almost as much as actually saying them.

He mused: If I make this point about the new role of
the central system early on, I won't have to worry about
someone interrupting my flow. Besides, that concept is
synergistic with current thinking in Purchase.

Hanrahan, Saranga, Casey, and Taradalsky all looked
to Purchase for guidance and inputs. Purchase had
become to these development VPs and their staffs what
Paris had been to the artists of the forties—a center for
leading-edge concepts and development.

Crawford discovered that his interpretation of the
new role of the centralized site mirrored the thinking
of the development VPs when he had reviewed it with
one of the assistants to Earl Wheeler, VP of Corporate
Programming and the head of the Purchase group. In
that meeting, Crawford had been strongly advised to
include the centralized host-based systems at the head
of any hierarchical presentation on the future role of
enterprise computing. The central resource must be in
there to make the networks work.

This reminded of him of what Digital Equipment's
Ken Olsen had said regarding this problem: "The problem is that everyone has been going about this backwards—buying lots of computers and then trying to
connect them together. We have to start thinking of
computers as peripherals. You start with the network,

then you hang the computers on later." This concept made a lot of sense.

Returning to his task, Crawford focused his eyes on his legal pad to address the next item—Dispersed Processing. If he were teaching a class, he thought, this might be the proper point to ask class members a question that would surely keep them awake: What is the difference between dispersed processing and distributed data processing?

Leaning back in his seat, he wondered how the MC members would define dispersed processing. How would they define distributed data processing? Would someone say that any time you disperse processing you also distribute data processing or whenever you distribute data processing you also disperse it? Was it possible that people might combine or confuse the two terms? If so, he would have a handful untangling them.

Crawford took a sip of his drink as he concentrated on how to clarify and distinguish between distributed data processing and dispersed processing. During his meetings over the last few weeks, he had discovered that people were basically comfortable with the idea that distributed data processing and dispersed processing had different meanings. However, he wondered how to introduce these concepts.

Many people have strong feelings about the meaning and history of the development of these concepts. If he walked into Digital Equipment Corporation and said, "You folks are the leaders in distributed data processing and you're an also-ran in dispersed processing," their faces would light up. And someone would proudly say, "That's right." But if he said to them, "You are an also-ran in distributed processing and the unquestionable

leader in dispersed processing," they would probably
ask him to leave.

He scribbled on his notepad:

> The minicomputer made it possible to dis-
> perse computing resources throughout a
> company.

He sipped his scotch and wondered whether that
statement was clear enough. Perhaps he should emphasize the point that the minicomputer made it possible
to disperse computing resources in the form of *stand-
alone systems throughout an enterprise.*

> Gentlemen, the emergence of the minicom-
> puter made possible the use of stand-alone
> systems for departmental data processing.

The use of *departmental* would limit the scope of his
remarks to medium and large enterprise environments
and omit small businesses. It was just too difficult to
talk about computing in the large enterprise and small
enterprise environment at the same time. He admon-
ished himself: Keep it simple.

Should he mention that IBM played a role in the
development of the minicomputer industry? In 1979,
IBM had introduced the Series/1 minicomputer. Since
then the company had sold a few billion dollars worth.
They also sold hundreds of thousands of small business
systems such as the System/32s, /34s, and /36s—more
small business systems than any other competitor.

Reviewing his train of thought, Crawford realized
that the term *minicomputer* has never really been
embraced within the company. *Minicomputer* is more a
competitor's term than IBM's.

By now, Crawford was highly irritated with himself. It was as if his mind had driven past a sign that read DEAD END, and continued full bore to the edge of an abyss.

Crawford believed that a trailhead marked the beginning of all, or at least most, paths of thought. Even when thick brush obscured the marker, it was still there. He had missed the marker.

Discouraged over his stalled progress, he started again. Suddenly something clicked. In a flickering moment of inspiration he saw in his mind's eye a trail marker that read, *Aficionado*. That's the path to take! These men of the MC all have something in common. They are all aficionados of computing. They don't need a big introduction to grasp the term *dispersed* processing.

He felt a great weight lifting off his shoulders. All he would have to say was:

> Dispersed processing places computer resources around an enterprise for requirements that are generally not suited for a centralized host-based system.

That's it. And the phrase *not suited for a centralized host-based system* would help set the stage for explaining the difference between *dispersed* processing and the really charged term, *distributed* data processing.

At this point, Carl took another sip of his drink and focused his mind on the more highly charged concept of *distributed* data processing. The best way to develop this definition, he decided, would be to recap some of IBM's distributed data processing experience.

At the beginning of the eighties, IBM received a shock. Several large banks stated that they wanted to install minicomputers throughout their home and branch offices. These banks wanted to disperse computer systems in a way different from stand-alone decentralized systems. And they wanted to connect the minicomputers via telecommunications to form a network.

In some cases, the banks had wanted to distribute the application programs, or parts of them, such as those that debited and credited customers' account files, to the minicomputers. Those programs traditionally resided on the centralized system. What if the banks had told IBM that they also wanted to replicate large chunks of the central site data base onto the minis? These data bases, of course, traditionally resided on the central site computer. The MC might have replied, "They can't take data off of the mainframe. It would destroy the proper hierarchy of computing. Don't let them do anything that could threaten our mainframe business, our disk storage business."

In Crawford's mind, the present members of the Management Committee had a liberal view of the distributing function of the centralized site. They believed, he thought, that with care you could distribute some function off the host, provided IBM had the products to distribute that function to. Otherwise someone else would get the business.

What the banks had wanted to do disturbed many IBMers. Their approach to placing computer systems around a corporation upset IBM, not just because it might threaten IBM's mainframe business, but because IBM had been working on a product called the 8100 that seemed to offer customers a rational approach to distributed data processing.

Crawford decided to briefly remind the committee of the reasons why IBM had decided to build the 8100.

Early Attempts at Distribution

In the second half of the seventies, IBM had sold large numbers of terminals and 3790 cluster controllers. Users plugged their terminals into the 3790, which in turn plugged into a 3705 front-end processor that performed communication and control functions between the terminals and the mainframe. The 3705 plugged internally into the centralized mainframe or host.

Customers had demanded a product that would distribute more resources down at the cluster controller level. The 3790s had neither adequate processing power, storage, nor software support to permit the distribution of even the most rudimentary applications from the mainframe. Routine data entry and information display were formidable tasks. Large users wanted more processing power to manage and control their terminals. IBM decided to build the 8100 to give them that distributed processing power.

The 8100 information system was a layered operating system based on a new architecture which provided common application services across a resource manager which allowed interactive, batch, and transaction processing. Primary users are end-user departments in branch offices, stores, hospitals, claims offices, and other locations remote from the central data processing site.

When IBM had the 8100 under development, it was also building the 4300 computer, which some people argued could be utilized as a dispersed computer to meet many of the banks' requirements. The 4300 was a communication subsystem that used the System/370 architecture and and was suited for commercial, office, interactive problem solving, and engineering/scientific applications. That was the time of the big war.

Carl reflected: The war—Systems Communications Division in Raleigh versus the Data Systems Division in New York. Extremely bitter war, too—even by IBM standards.

The Communication Products Division people argued that their 3790 had to be replaced. They felt strongly that the 8100, then under development, was critically needed and that it would meet the growing requirement for distributed data processing products. Some argued that substantial money had been invested in the development of the 8100.

The data processing people, on the other side, were convinced the 8100 was inadequate to compete against minicomputers for distributed processing as they saw it. They argued that the E–Series (4300), which was about to be announced with a substantially improved price/ performance ratio, was what was needed to combat the whole emerging trend toward minicomputers.

Both sides won the battle. In 1979 IBM announced the 8100, complete with two operating systems—DPCX, which effectively permitted the 8100 to replace the 3790, and DPPX, which theoretically permitted the customer to build distributed networks. The 8100 with DPCX enabled IBM to provide users with more so-called *dis-tributing* processing capability than the 3790 could. The trade press heralded the 8100 as an indication that IBM was finally *taking the plunge into distributed processing*.

Several members of the Management Committee reportedly gulped and felt the system should never have been announced. They believed that the 8100 did not provide enough processing power, disk storage, or software to swim in the mainstream of distributed processing. Many maverick IBM customers could have become carried away with the 8100 and ported applications. As it turned out, almost all the 8100s sold served as cluster controllers.

After clarifying the 8100 issue, Carl decided that he would explain what distributed data processing encompassed by quoting from the IBM *Dictionary of Computing*:

> (1) Data processing in which some or all of the processing, storage, and control functions, in addition to input/output functions, are dispersed among data processing stations. (2) Data processing in which application transaction programs distributed among interconnected processors cooperate to perform distributed applications for end users of a network.

At least that portion of his presentation was now clear to him.

Suddenly, through the plane's loudspeaker, the flight attendant advised passengers to fasten their seatbelts. The plane was beginning its descent into La Guardia.

Crawford had not realized so much time had passed. He would have to finish the last part of this presentation in his hotel room that evening—that didn't leave him much time. He wondered whether he would see Saranga, Casey, Hanrahan, and Taradalsky again.

Maybe, if he were lucky, he'd be permitted to stay for Earl Wheeler's presentation.

At precisely this same hour on the following day, Crawford was pacing back and forth in the Management Committee anteroom.

4 Milford, Connecticut

FEBRUARY 18, 1987—7:00 A.M.

IBM employment records list him as Myron Saranga, but nearly everyone calls him Mike or Saranga.

On this Wednesday morning, Mike Saranga left his Connecticut home and drove for a few minutes on secondary roads before turning on to the Merritt Parkway. Rather than heading northeast toward his Milford, Connecticut, office as he usually would, Saranga headed southwest toward New York. Today his schedule, like Hanrahan's, included a morning meeting at Purchase and an afternoon meeting with the MC.

Before entering the state of New York, Saranga paid the 35-cent fee at the last Connecticut tollbooth. At this point, the Merritt Parkway becomes the Hutchinson River Parkway, and Connecticut law meets New York law. Saranga drove through the tollbooth, and within a few minutes, left the Hutchinson River Parkway at Exit 37.

Saranga, a man with strong facial features that might be considered handsome, has a dark complexion and deep black hair. He is about five feet eleven inches tall, is of medium build, and speaks with a New England accent. He is a complex human being.

Like Dick Hanrahan, Saranga too has an impressive title—General Manager of Software Development—and a management position in the IBM programming community. However, while Hanrahan works for the IBM group that manufactures personal computers, Saranga reports to IBM Information Services (IIS), an independent business unit within IBM's sales and marketing division that provides remote computer services. While Hanrahan concentrates on the development of personal computer software, especially the needs of the PS/2, Saranga focuses on application programs across all major IBM product lines.

Application Programs

Some say that programs such as Ashton-Tate's dBASE III®, Lotus 1–2–3®, and SuperCalc®3 are application programs. Wrong, wrong, and wrong again. They are not application programs—despite the fact that personal computer users call them application programs.

The definition of an "application program" taken from the *The Dictionary of Computing* (Oxford University Press, 1983) is as follows:

> Any program that is specific to the particular role that a given computer performs within a given organization and makes a direct contribution to performing that role. For exam-

ple, where a computer handles a company's finances, a payroll program would be an application program. By contrast, an operating system and a software tool may both be essential to the effective use of the computer system, but neither makes a direct contribution to meeting the end user's eventual needs.

The phrase "makes a direct contribution to meeting the end user's eventual needs" is key to understanding the essence of application programs. Data base management systems and spreadsheets are usually subsets of a larger program—the application program—that makes a direct contribution to the end user's eventual needs. dBASE III®, Lotus 1-2-3®, and SuperCalc®3 are application enabling programs/software tools. They do not entirely meet the end user's eventual needs.

Word processing programs such as MicroPro's excellent WordStar™ Professional 4.0 fit the definition better, and so do desktop publishing systems like Aldus's PageMaker® and computer-aided publishing programs like Frame Technology Corporation's Frame Maker™. These programs are true application programs. Word-Star™ Professional 4.0 enables users to prepare a finished letter, document, or report. Aldus's PageMaker® allows users to prepare entire brochures, manuals, or reports. With Frame Maker™, users can prepare a manuscript like the one for this book. Word processing, publishing systems, payroll, and manufacturing resource planning are all application programs. This distinction enables us to understand what Saranga and his team were working on.

Computer Vendors Watch

Executives of computer companies try to figure out just what direction Saranga's organization will take because application programs are to computers what video cassettes are to VCRs. The videos sell VCRs. Application programs sell computers. The more application programs that are available for a particular company's computers, the more computers that company will sell.

All computer makers—AT&T, Apple, Altos Computer, Compaq, Data General, DEC, Epson, Fujitsu, and HP included—recognize that fact. Every one of them wants to have *all* the available application programs running on their computers. They don't like to see any application programs except the really bad ones running on their competitors' hardware. IBM is no different. It wants all the good application programs to be supported on its computers—not on the competitors' products.

Other manufacturers watch carefully to determine how IBM will go about increasing the number of application programs that can run on IBM machines. They try to determine how Saranga's group motivates the software companies—those that support Apple's, AT&T's, DEC's, HP's, Wang's, and dozens of other computer manufacturers' products—to switch to IBM.

Software Company Concerns

Curiosity alone does not explain why so many software companies are concerned with the plans laid down by Saranga's department. That has to do with the battle for software markets. It has to do with wanting to win, and it has to do with preserving a company's status, identity, and position. It also has to do with the tremendous opportunities that IBM can create for software vendors.

J. R. R. Tolkien wrote in *The Hobbit*: "Do not make decisions that affect the dragon, if the dragon lives near you." IBM is certainly not a dragon—unless, perhaps, you are a direct competitor—but it is a powerful force. Software companies live, unavoidably, near that force —some closer than others, some perhaps nearer than they prefer. Those software executives don't want to make uninformed decisions when they are jousting with a better-than-fifty-billion-dollar beast. Mike Saranga's direction, with respect to software, is to a large extent the direction of the beast.

The decisions made by Saranga and his group affect more than just "application program" companies. They also affect software companies in the other three software product segments: application enabling programs/software tools, communications programs, and

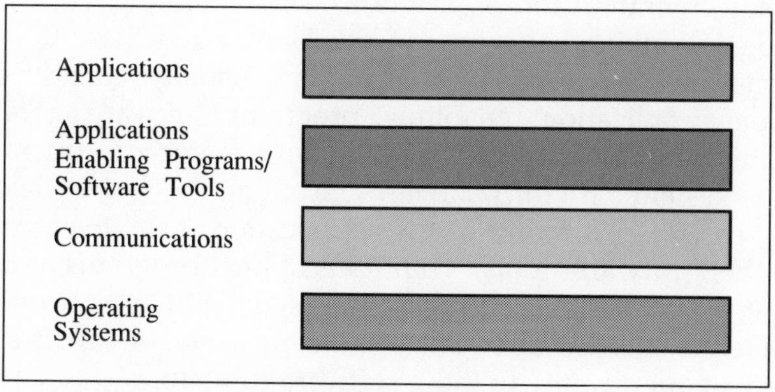

Figure 1 – Software Product Segments or Layers

operating systems. These four segments are shown in Figure 1.

A decision made at the applications layer has a domino effect on the three segments or "layers" below. When Saranga's group decided to remarket Hogan System's banking application programs, other suppliers of application programs for the banking industry had to adjust to that decision. They had to consider what might happen to them if the IBM sales and marketing organizations were really aggressive about selling that product. Then Hogan banking software, i.e., IBM/Hogan banking software, would become a much greater competitive threat. And the story doesn't end with developers of application programs.

When Hogan and IBM announced their alliance, some software companies in the application enabling programs/software tools segment of the market quickly asked what application enabling programs/software tools—data base management system, languages, and so on—the Hogan banking program used. The communications software and operating system developers asked what communications programs and operating systems Hogan banking software ran on. They asked these questions because application programs usually consist of some application enabling programs/software tools, some communications software, and a specific operating system. If IBM/Hogan's banking software sales increased significantly, the application enabling programs/software tools, communications programs, and operating systems programs used with it would increase in sales also. Such shifts present both a threat and an opportunity to those software companies.

Let's look at a second, more significant example—IBM's plan to offer a series of office application programs—that impacts a broader range of software suppliers in all four software segments. In late 1986 some software companies realized that IBM planned to develop office applications for the PS/2, which had not been announced yet, and that those office applications would utilize IBM's own data base management system, also under development. Once those applications became available, assuming that customers bought them, not many people would need to purchase a data base management system for their PS/2. And if IBM were to sell millions of these systems, suppliers of the communications programs that link into data bases would surely be affected. They would have to provide communications programs that work with that installed base. Sales of millions of PS/2s with the OS/2 operating system would undoubtedly impact all operating systems companies' business. Most users who purchase a PS/2 system with an OS/2 operating system would immediately become a poorer prospect to computer companies that sell UNIX, Pick, or some other operating system.

For good or for bad, the decisions made by Saranga's department impact software providers in all four segments of the software industry. That does not mean that decisions made at the other three layers have no effect on Saranga. Not at all. They do. Decisions made about software by other IBM executives and other software companies at any segment could influence or even dictate many of Saranga's organization's decisions. It's a two-way street to the multi-billion-dollar software market.

Saranga's Background

Saranga began his IBM career in Poughkeepsie, New York. There, as a young man, IBM presented him with his first major opportunity and a great challenge—to work on the development of MVS, the batch processing operating system for the 370 family of computers.

The MVS operating system controls IBM's biggest System/370s. It is the largest and most developed operating system in existence, and most of the largest corporations in the world, at least in the United States, run on it.

When Saranga arrived in Poughkeepsie, millions of lines of code had to be written, tested, and debugged. The complexity of MVS was overwhelming. Some questioned whether it would ever work at all. During that wild time, Mike Saranga became a key part of the MVS project and worked his way up to MVS Systems Product Manager.

Second Opportunity

In 1977 the corporation offered Saranga his second big opportunity—to participate in the development of a computer program that could potentially change how people use computers. IBM offered him the job of managing ongoing development of the first data base management system for the System/360—the Information Management System, or IMS, as management information system departments refer to it.

By 1974, just 10 years after the introduction of the System/360, every large company *had* to own one. But as soon as the customer implemented several applications on the system, a major problem developed—data could not be effectively managed. Some personal computer users in the early eighties experienced a similar problem. Many more will experience it as they, too, implement multiple applications on their PCs. Fortunately, the concepts, technology, and products have already been developed to solve this problem. That was not the case, however, in the early seventies.

In the early seventies, the customers, IBM, and other computer vendors thought of an application, such as payroll, as two separate and specific parts—a program and a data file. Any application had a program and specific data file. Figure 2 illustrates this relationship.

Each pair of circles represents an application. Each application consists of part program and part data. What is key here is that the program and the file are in effect linked together. That is where the problem lies.

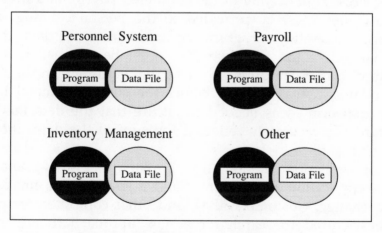

Figure 2 – Program/Data File Relationship Before IMS

When users began to implement several applications, they discovered one hell of a problem—the data of one application became dependent on the data of a second application. Let's look at a company that implements a computerized payroll application and a computerized shop floor cost accounting application. A separate program and a separate data file accompany each application.

This system works fine until the company implements a third application—for example, an inventory management application—that uses data from both data files. The problem is not that the data for the third application, which is the sum of the data of the first two files, requires an investment in additional storage capabilities. The problem occurs in file updating, or lack of it.

The customer runs the shop floor cost accounting program again and again. Meanwhile, the data in the payroll file and the inventory are changing in a separate process. A new copy of the combined payroll and inventory files must be provided to the person running the cost accounting program, or each piece of data that changed in the first two files must be changed in the third file. Regardless of how the customer made the updates, it was a mess. Before the customer knew it, a virtual army was needed to ensure that the data in the third file accurately reflected the sum of the data in the first two files.

It was apparent that this approach to thinking about an application as a program and a specific data file had to change. Customers, IBM, and other computer companies started to search for a new approach to applications. They came up with the idea that the program section of the application could remain separate, but that the collective data used by the programs could be treated as a single entity, a data bank. All programs would access the same data from the same bank. This would, its designers hoped, eliminate the redundancy and synchronization problem. Figure 3 demonstrates this new outlook on the program/data relationship.

This was a great innovation, but as soon as people began to think in terms of a centralized or corporate data base, they realized that the technology for a data base management system needed to be developed. That's where IMS comes in.

Two approaches combined to lay the groundwork for the development of IMS. These occurred before Saranga arrived in California. The first effort was led by

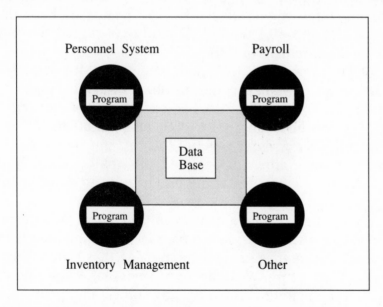

Figure 3 – New Outlook on the Program/Data File Relationship

IBM's Santa Teresa Labs' Uri Berman, who was then an IBM Systems Engineer at North American Rockwell. Berman defined the concept and technology to provide improved control of the corporate data resource, data independence from individual applications, and application data sharing. He subsequently designed and implemented his theory in a system that became the DL/I data base system. Concurrently, IBM was studying the long-term direction and usage of the rapidly expanding Direct Access Storage Device (DASD) and the difficulty customers were having defining and using data stored on DASD. Study results indicated that the time had come for development of a general-purpose data base technology. The study also concluded that one prerequisite for the introduction of a data base is an environment for storing and managing data communications/transactions efficiently. The results of Berman's work and those of the DASD study converged, leading to the development of IMS.

When offered the 1977 assignment of IMS Data Systems Product Manager and an office on Sand Hill Road in Menlo Park, California, Saranga immediately accepted. He and his family packed themselves off to the San Francisco Bay Area. It was not the pleasant Bay Area climate or the rolling, oak-spotted hills that enticed him. He did not want to miss the opportunity to work at the cutting edge of data base technology.

By the time Saranga arrived in California, the company had long since decided to base IMS's design on a hierarchical file management structure. At that time, a hierarchical structure was the only one that made sense. However, neither IBM nor any other company had much experience developing such a system. The process of developing the 700,000 lines of code that existed before Saranga's arrival had not been smooth. False starts, bug-infested code, and lethargic program modules led many developers to believe that the project was jinxed. A serious morale problem was festering.

But IMS was not the only morale problem. Two years prior to Saranga's arrival in California, IBM management decided to build a West Coast programming lab where all Bay Area IBM programmers could work under one roof. However, the company had decided not to build it near the General Product's Division facilities in the Menlo Park and Palo Alto area of the peninsula where most of the programmers lived, but in the southernmost part of San Jose (practically near Los Angeles to hear IBMers describe it). Everyone was livid. Few people wanted to move from the northern Bay Area to San Jose. Some towns south of the lab like Morgan Hill still didn't have sidewalks on many streets. Despite verbal and written complaints, the company built the lab—the now-famous Santa Teresa Labs—anyway. The programmers had been interned in the new Santa Teresa facilities for only a few months when Saranga arrived. Many of them were not pleased.

The relocation problems, exacerbated by the IMS problems, created an explosive environment. Not too long after Saranga's arrival, one of the programmers wrote him a blistering memo. The memo informed Saranga that his approach to some aspect of IMS was all wrong. The critic certainly couldn't have any idea how Saranga would respond—neither Saranga nor his rich sense of humor were so well known throughout the IBM programming community at that time. But a couple of days later, the programmer received Saranga's reply. It

read that the programmer had a serious problem—someone was signing his name to dumb memos
and would he find out who was doing it and put a stop
to it. Some IBMers felt the programmer was damn
lucky; another exec might have sent him packing.

Saranga could do nothing about raising people's
morale over the relocation issue. In fact, a few months
after he settled into the Palo Alto area, he discovered
that his own office would be at the new Santa Teresa
Labs. He didn't approve—he would have preferred liv-
ing near Stanford University in Palo Alto. Neither did
Saranga approve of the basic design of the Santa Teresa
Labs. The architecture was not traditional enough for
his taste. But regardless of his personal preferences,
Saranga was there to get a job done, and he recognized
the importance of raising morale in the areas over
which he had some control.

Saranga tried many approaches to improve the
morale problem of the IMS workers. His most celebrat-
ed one was a vanity license plate. He bought a California license plate with IMS #1 on it, then put it on his
car and parked the car conspicuously in front of the
entrance where the IMS programmers entered and left
the building. He hoped that sight of the plate would
remind the IMS programmers that they were working
on the lab's #1 project. He hoped that it would elevate
their spirits.

Saranga must have made more good decisions than
bad ones, otherwise IBM would not have allowed him
to run the show for roughly five years. He must have
made some right decisions, because during his tenure
the IMS lines of code grew from 700,000 to more than

one million. Those additional lines of code made it possible for IBM to market IMS as a high-performance,
high-availability, high-capacity data base management
system for critical operations such as on-line banking,
airline reservations and other transaction-oriented
applications. When Saranga arrived at the Santa Teresa
Labs, IMS had a few hundred customers. When he left,
it had more than 2,000. By 1987, more than 6,500 IMS
users, all large enterprises, around the world relied on
its capabilities daily to meet their data management and
data communications requirements, making IMS one
of IBM's greatest software product revenue generators.

Third Opportunity

Before Saranga left California, he seized yet another
important opportunity. Just up the road from the Santa
Teresa Labs, the real long-haired IBM techies hang out
at IBM San Jose Research, where they work on esoteric
projects. This advanced research facility has no direct
ties to the Santa Teresa Labs. What was important was
that IBM San Jose Research developed the concepts and
structure for an approach to managing data that was
totally different from the IMS hierarchical approach to
data files. San Jose Research had developed a relational
model and a prototype data base management system
based on that model. The prototype was called System
R.

Around 1979, IBM top management sensed that San
Jose Research just might have made a great technologi-

cal breakthrough, and the relational technology was transferred to Santa Teresa. That gave Saranga his third big opportunity—the chance to take the cutting-edge relational technology and help create DB2, a relational data base.

The relational concepts held the promise of a breakthough in computing as significant as the concepts that led to the creation of corporate data banks. Relational systems held the promise of enabling programs to think of data not just as records of information but as tables of information. It held the promise of allowing a program to manage, access, and control great quantities of data with only a few lines of code. For IMS or other record-processing and hierarchically structured data bases to do the same, hundreds—sometimes thousands—of lines of code would be required. For this and other reasons, the development of a relational data base management system represented an opportunity to advance the state of computing.

By 1986 the world computer industry had long since recognized the importance of relational technology. Thousands of customers were using DB2, another of IBM's most successful program products.

The Three Lead to a Fourth

A fourth opportunity—possibly the most important—arose before Saranga left Santa Teresa. It appeared, not in the form of another product development opportunity, but in the form of a man.

Around 1980, an IBM executive from Kingston, New York, Earl Wheeler, visited the Santa Teresa Labs. He asked Saranga for some help. Had Saranga failed to recognize this opportunity, he would never have been invited to this morning's meeting at the IBM Corporate Staff Headquarters or to the afternoon Management Committee meeting in Armonk, New York.

5 Stouffers—White Plains, New York

FEBRUARY 17, 1987—7:45 P.M.

Carl Crawford arrived at La Guardia, walked to the baggage area, and touched a button that dialed the Connecticut Limousine Service. Ten to fifteen minutes later, a blue stretch limo whisked him and several other occupants north. An hour or so later, he paid the driver $15 and quickly checked into Stouffers, a favorite hotel of many IBM executives when they visit IBM headquarters.

The front-desk clerk gave him a message from the Administrative Assistant who had first set up the next day's meeting. Crawford stuffed the message into his pocket. There was something he wanted to do before he returned the call.

Just the previous week the AA had finally confided to Crawford that Earl Wheeler and the four divisional

programming Vice Presidents—Hanrahan, Saranga,
Casey, and Taradalsky—would announce a plan having
something to do with cooperative processing at tomorrow afternoon's MC meeting. That information
intrigued Crawford. It also influenced the sequence he
would follow in his presentation. He decided to start off
with centralized processing, followed by dispersed and
distributed processing, and end strongly with cooperative processing.

He rushed off to his room to complete the cooperative processing section of his presentation before he
called the AA back. Surely, he thought, the AA hadn't
called just to make sure his plane had come down soft-
ly; he called to make sure that Crawford had his
thoughts clear on all points of the presentation, especially cooperative processing.

Crawford removed four mounted overheads from
his briefcase. He had decided back in Rochester that he
would use them to help report on the common usage
throughout IBM of the term *cooperative processing*. The
first overhead (Figure 1) described the overall scope and
benefits of cooperative processing. He had decided that
when this slide was projected onto the MC conference
room screen, he would begin with the statement:
"Cooperative processing is an all-encompassing process." He had clearly written that sentence in his notes.
It would provide him with the lead-in he needed to
develop his topic adequately.

His eyes focused on the center of the diagram. The
abbreviation APPL in the center of the slide would trigger the word *applications*, and the key words in the APPL
quadrant would help him formulate the next key sentence. Tomorrow he would remark: "In a cooperative

processing environment, users should be able to run any type of application, from any source, anytime." He had written that down in his notes.

When he looked at the abbreviation INFO, he knew the word *information* would come to mind. The other key words in that block would help him create the sentence: "In a cooperative processing environment, all types of information must be accommodated." He would then read off the types of information—voice, data, video, and imaging. He would be sure to continue with: "The system must be able to facilitate all types of information coming from all points in the network." He jotted a note to himself to remember to make the

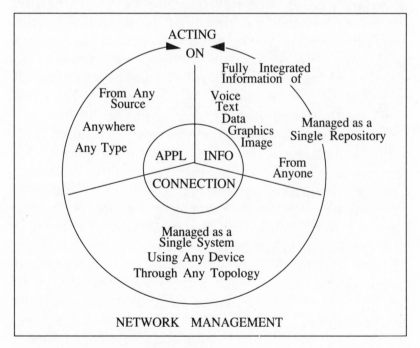

Figure 1 – Cooperative Processing

point that a central repository would keep track of the characteristics of each user, including location, type of equipment, and other information, to help make a cooperative processing environment possible.

The associations he had made with the word *Connection* and the key words in that area of the slide easily brought to mind his practiced rhetoric: "In a cooperative environment, through any topology—including hierarchical, peer-to-peer, or hybrids of the two—every device must be connected, and all connections must be managed as a single system."

Those sentences would be enough, he thought, to trigger other related points. He would elaborate on them when and where necessary. He also made a note that just before taking this figure down he should say: "In a cooperative processing environment, users have access to all the computer network facilities they need to do their work. The user need not be concerned with which computer in the network is performing the processing or where that computer resource is physically located." He wrote down another good thought: "The user does not have to know where his application program or his data reside in the network. The entire computer resource should be transparent to the user. Basically, the network with all its complexity should be hidden from the user." With that he hastened on to the next figure and the next key point of cooperative processing.

In introducing this point he would say: "If we stand back and think about what functions a cooperative processing environment provides to a user, we see they can be lumped into four basic functions—processing, storage, communications, and management." Again, tomorrow he would elaborate on this statement.

His next point would state that: "A tremendous amount of hardware and software, all working together, is needed to perform those functions for every user in a cooperative processing environment." Once he mentioned *hardware,* he knew he could start getting back down to the real world.

He fixed in his mind that at this point in the presentation he would say: "Gentlemen, over the years we have used the term *cooperative processing* to encompass how more than one computer can work together to meet customers' requirements." He knew that when he mentioned *more than one computer,* the members would collectively associate the IBM entry-level computers, the IBM midrange computers, and the IBM high-end or mainframe computers.

Entry-level systems consist of the personal computers based on the Intel chip and Microsoft's operating system that IBM first announced in November 1981. This category also includes the Personal System/2 family, which was scheduled to be announced on April 2, 1987.

The midrange consists of the System/36 and System/38 families of computers. The /36 and the /38 are two very different animals, designed for different user requirements. The /36 was designed for small business users who did not want or could not afford their own computer operators and programmers. Machine users cannot easily change things around or optimize the system. The IBM sales force later sold /36s to larger corporations that needed a computer in a department, main office, or a remote branch. The /38, on the other hand, is a highly advanced system best utilized by someone who really knows how to maximize the use of the computer. The /38 offers a 48-bit addressing scheme and a relational data base. These two product lines, with different operating systems, still comprised IBM's midrange product line in 1987.

The high-end computer, the mainframe, consists of the 370 family that includes several models: the 9370, the 4300, and the 3090. They run operating systems such as MVS, MVS/XA, VM, and VSE.

Now Crawford decided he would state: "The three families must work together to provide those four basic functions of cooperative processing—processing, storing, input/output, as well as overall control or management of the system." He knew that none of the families really worked well together. Some competitors would say it was even unusual for models within the same IBM family to work together. But he had known for several years now that IBM had been working hard to improve the situation, and some progress had been made. He speculated that if IBM ever expected to make cooperative processing a reality, it would have to continue that advancement.

He decided to relate the different computer families to the different functions required for a cooperative processing environment: "Although all the computers in each of the families provide the four basic functions we have just discussed, each of the families plays a special role in the cooperative processing environment." He figured the members of the MC would realize where he was headed.

At this point he would display the next figure (Figure 2). His accompanying text would be: "The entry-level system products, primarily the personal computers serving as workstations, are best suited for the input/output function. They allow the user to access the systems and all its users and resources. The workstation becomes an extension of the centralized mainframe as well as an extension of the other computers on the network. It becomes an extension of the entire system's resources."

Now that he had addressed the special role of the entry-level product in a cooperative processing environment, the moment would be ripe to discuss the special role of the high-end product in a cooperative environment. Crawford decided not to focus on the role of the centralized mainframe but concentrate on the role of the smallest 370—the 9370. He decided to begin: "We all know that the IBM computer families—the entry-level system, the midrange, and the mainframe—provide processing resources in a cooperative environment. Those families of computers help

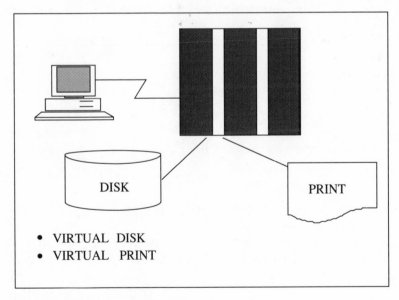

Figure 2 – Extensions of Resources

meet the users' needs for processing power. However, we also know that users will intensify their needs for processing resources as they run increasingly complex programs. Users will need to progressively distribute some applications off the centralized mainframe. The 9370 is the ideal computer to upload programs that are too complex for the workstation and to download programs that don't require the resources of the centralized mainframe. The 9370 provides a large part of the additional processing resources that will be needed throughout the network in a cooperative processing environment. It's the *processing* engine in our cooperative processing environment."

To help get this point across, Crawford would support it with Figure 3. He also made a note to give additional examples of how the 9370 provides processing resources in this environment. He wrote: "Information

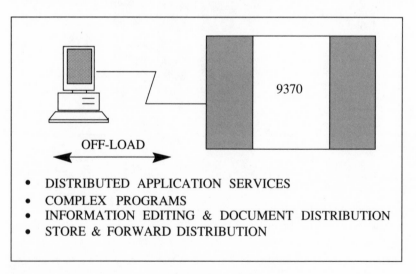

Figure 3 – Off-loading to Another Processor

editing and document distribution can be performed by the 9370. Electronic publishing has given information editing new meaning that goes far beyond word processing." He was fairly confident that the MC would know exactly what he meant.

Next he would comment on the IBM computer model within the midrange family that had been designated to meet users' needs to store and retrieve the huge amounts of data implicit in a cooperative processing environment. Carl Crawford knew a lot more about this machine than he did about the entry-level or the high-end systems. For over two years the company had been developing the 3X follow-on product at the facility where he worked in Rochester, Minnesota. He wrote the following key sentence: "The new S/3X, the follow-on product to the System/36 and /38, has been designated not only as the growth-path machine for /36 and /38 customers, but as the data base engine in a cooperative processing environment." He contemplated elaborating on this point by stating: "The S/3X is being built with the same extended addressing as the /38. That extended addressing will give the S/3X greater flexibility in addressing data and will make the S/3X ideal as a distributed data base machine in a cooperative processing environment."

IBM, thought Carl, is well aware that it needs to provide its System/36 customers in particular a means to migrate up to more powerful and effective computers. System/36 users who've outgrown their systems cannot easily move up to either the /38 or the mainframe products. To do so would mean a massive investment to rewrite their application's software, convert their data, and retrain everyone on the new system. The same problem exists for /38 users although few of them are *maxed out* at this time. The new S/3X holds that promise of an economical migration path for both customer bases. However, for a cooperative computing environment to have any hope of becoming a reality, a computer that can help manage and access data that is located on different computers throughout the network is badly needed. Crawford mused: I see the S/3X becoming the *distributed data base* engine in a cooperative processing environment.

Crawford wrote the following key sentence: "The new S/3X has been designated as the source of distributed data bases. Store-and-forward distribution of information from the intermediate processor rather than point-to-point workstation networks have obvious advantages." Store-and-forward refers to the system's capability to store messages and then forward them to the

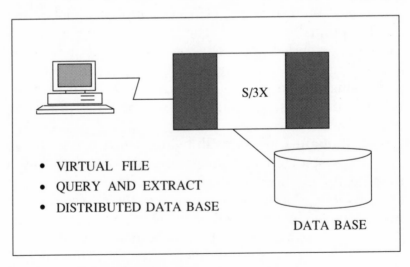

Figure 4 – Access to Distributed Data

appropriate destination. Large personal or work-unit data bases can be stored and/or backed up on the processor (virtual file). Essential data base administration functions and services for distributed data bases (controlling and scheduling distribution from mainframe data bases, directory, dictionary maintenance, etc.) can be performed at that level, relieving the user of this responsibility. Crawford would use Figure 4 to help him develop the point that the midrange S/3X would provide the additional data storage requirement of a cooperative processing environment.

That's it, I'm finished, he thought to himself. He decided to end cleanly by summarizing: "You asked me to present comments on several important computer concepts that enable us to think clearly about the business we are in, concepts such as centralized, dispersed, distributed, and cooperative processing. I have related the different IBM families of computers to the basic functions of a cooperative environment. This information represents the general thinking of people throughout our organization. Now, if you have any questions, I will attempt to answer them." With that he tossed his pencil high up in the air and leaned back in the chair.

At just about the time the pencil hit the floor, the phone rang. Crawford answered it, and heard the AA ask, "Where the hell have you been?" Not waiting for an answer, he ran on: "I've got a crisis on my hands, and I don't like having to spend my time tracking you down!"

Crawford made the usual apology for not calling the second he arrived at the hotel. The AA pointed out that although he was very pressed for time that evening, he had a directive to review all the key points of Carl's speech. Carl realized the AA was probably following orders from his superiors, so he attempted to comply with the AA's request.

After he finished his run-through for the AA, which took about half an hour, the AA informed him that two points bothered him. Both related to cooperative processing. The AA told Crawford not to oversell it. Emphasize that cooperative processing is a long-range strategic goal. That today, in the real world, it's little more than a gleam in someone's eye. Point out that this is something we are working toward. That will assure the MC that you have your feet on the ground.

His second point was to downplay transparency. The MC knows that real transparency is unlikely ever to be achieved in a generic sense. They get nervous when anyone says that transparency is here or just over the hill.

Crawford agreed with the AA on both points. He assured him that he would present a more realistic picture of cooperative processing and transparency. To himself he thought that the AA's feedback had been a bit brusque, but he had to agree that the content was right on.

Before ending the conversation, Crawford made a point to ask how his remarks on cooperative processing jibed with those that Wheeler and his team were giving in the afternoon. It was the wrong time to question the AA.

Annoyed, the AA told Crawford not to worry about the afternoon. "What's happening tomorrow has to do with a lot more things than just cooperative processing. Besides, Wheeler doesn't go over his speech with anyone."

The AA rambled on for a few more seconds and then abruptly hung up. Before hanging up, however, he mumbled something to the effect that he hoped that Carl actually got to go on. It seemed that whatever the big crisis was, it might pre-empt his presentation.

Crawford tried to recall what the AA had said: "We've got a possible crisis on our hands. We've got a potentially big problem in Raleigh, you know—where Casey is headquartered. The MC may want to review the Raleigh situation. Sorry, I've got to go. I've got to find the Raleigh Mayor's home phone number and call him. Maybe he can tell us how bad a problem we have on our hands." That, to the best of Carl Crawford's recollection, was the AA's last statement.

6 Raleigh, North Carolina

Three North Carolina landmarks—the great Gothic Tower on Duke University's West Campus in Durham, the Old Well at the University of North Carolina at Chapel Hill, and the Memorial Bell Tower of North Carolina State University at Raleigh—have more in common than bricks and mortar. They form a large triangle with sides of 8, 12, and 14 miles. The focal point of that triangle is a body of 5,500 acres of gently rolling hills called Research Triangle Park—a complex devoted to research activities. The city of Raleigh, once known almost exclusively for textile and tobacco products, sits at the southernmost point of the triangle.

When most people in Raleigh hear the name *Avery*, they assume you are talking about Avery Upchurch. In these parts there is only one Avery, the Mayor of Raleigh and proprietor of the institution known as Upchurch Oil Service Company.

On February 18, Avery Upchurch awoke from a restless sleep, grabbed the clock, saw that it read 5:45 A.M., and then bolted to the bedroom window. Placing his face against the cold glass, he looked out onto his backyard and what had caused him to toss and turn throughout the night—the worst ice storm to hit the area in 30 years.

Upchurch had gone to sleep about 11 P.M. the night before. After a dozen phone calls, he had stopped answering the phone, which explains why IBM's Administrative Assistant in Armonk could not get through to him. Upchurch would later say that he thought the best thing he could do for the people was to get some sleep. His hands were tied. There was nothing he could do. He needed his rest to meet the challenges he'd face in the morning.

The storm had hit the Raleigh–Durham area on Monday, February 16. By early evening, it had forced the area to shut down. The Governor ordered the state police to emergency status and made them and their vehicles available to state legislators who needed to travel on state business. Anyone who stayed up that night watching the fall of ice knew that schools and industry would be frozen shut on Tuesday. On Tuesday morning, the storm continued to rage.

Near Raleigh, in Research Triangle Park, stand the long, white buildings of the IBM Communications Products Division (CPD). The third floor of Building 4 houses the office of Don Casey, Vice President of Programming.

CPD plays a significant role in IBM's business. Closing it, especially for more than a few days, could create a crisis at IBM. Its products are a part of just about every

IBM shipment—either they are individual parts in an integrated product or they are the *glue* that makes all the other parts of the system work. The Armonk AA was worried that the storm might impact CPD's ability to provide other IBM divisions with the parts they needed to fill orders.

The parts of the information systems that CPD manufactures are hardware products such as displays, terminals, modems, concentrators, local area networks (LANs), and other equipment generally referred to as telecommunications equipment. (The prefix *tele* is used because many of CPD's products enable customers to transmit data over the public telephone or private telecommunication networks.) These parts make up the communications hardware that customers use to access a host computer. Depending on the configuration, the parts could represent 25% of the system's purchase price. If a customer's order requires these parts and IBM runs out of stock, the entire order most likely will be held up.

The *glue* that CPD produces is the communications software. Communications software controls the access and flow of information from one piece of a hardware–software system to another. It ties the discrete elements together to form a system—a computer/communications network. Much of the communications software that CPD develops has a brand name—Systems Network Architecture.

SNA, that body of programs, rules, and conventions that enables IBM's terminals and computer products to interconnect, defines the logical structure, formats, protocols, and operational sequences for transmitting information units through, and for controlling, the config-

uration of computer networks. It is one of the computer industry's greatest achievements. Many of the largest
banks, brokerage houses, government agencies, insurance companies, retailers, manufacturers, universities,
and utilities around the world rely daily on one or
more of the 30,000 SNA networks that were in operation by the beginning of 1987. Hundreds of computer
and communications companies, such as Amdahl,
AT&T, DEC, Fujitsu, General Telephone, Hewlett–
Packard, other IBM divisions, ICL, Siemens, and Wang
Laboratories, just to mention a few, provide thousands
of SNA–compatible products and services.

CPD is the only IBM division to have a woman president, Ellen Hancock. Gray–haired, pleasant looking,
and pleasant speaking, Hancock is no paper-pushing,
know-nothing administrator. On the contrary, she is a
technical giant in what still is a highly technical, male
world. She stays on top of every communications technology issue affecting IBM. Both she and Casey have an
extraordinary grasp of the SNA technology. It's safe to
say that top management of IBM wants someone who
understands the technology running CPD.

However, neither Hancock nor anyone else at IBM
had the power to do anything about Raleigh's storm.
Even if Raleigh could clear the public roads, no one
could find a way to clear the five or six inches of ice
from CPD's private roads. CPD's Research Triangle Park
facility did not own any snow- or ice-removing equipment. Equipment would have to be flown in at huge
expense. Even if IBM were willing to support the cost, it
couldn't do it without an open airport.

That raised the second question on the AA's mind:
Was Don Casey able to leave the Raleigh area before the

storm hit? He would have had to leave before Monday to beat the storm.

The AA anticipated that the Management Committee would want to know about the Raleigh situation in the morning. He also suspected that Casey's absence might affect the MC's afternoon schedule, so he wanted as much notice as possible of a potential no-show.

Since Casey had worked with Earl Wheeler for over a year now on a plan that might have at least as big an impact on the world as SNA—one that might require $10 billion in R&D expenditures over the next 5 years—the AA thought Wheeler might request a postponement of the final launch meeting if one of his four generals failed to make the last checkoff meeting. Would Eisenhower have postponed the Normandy invasion if Montgomery, Bradley, or Taylor had failed to attend the last critical meeting? Who knows? The absence of one of the key generals might have been enough reason to postpone the meeting until the next favorable tide. Perhaps Casey's absence would be just enough reason for Wheeler to seek a postponement.

On that Tuesday night, the Armonk AA considered calling Ellen Hancock's Connecticut home to alert her to the possibility that Casey might be stuck in Raleigh and to inquire whether she might represent him at the two meetings. After reflecting that Hancock and Casey usually stay in close contact, that Casey and Wheeler had stayed in touch with each other for over a year, and that Hanock and Wheeler themselves maintained good lines of communication, he reconsidered. The odds were good that Hancock already knew whether Casey was stuck in Raleigh. If she decided to take Casey's place, she probably had a copy of Wheeler's plans, at least the part describing what Casey and CPD planned to do, and was studying it.

Don Casey is Ellen Hancock's glue man. He is responsible for programming CPD's communications software and for managing the highly technical group of code writers who enrich and expand the capabilities of SNA. He directs hundreds of CPD programmers who develop the software that enables broadband LANs, PBXs (Private Branch Exchanges), personal computers, midrange 3X computers, and 370 systems to communicate, and he develops the network management software, such as NetView, that customers use to manage those networks. Casey keeps the communications software glue spreading and sticking over all IBM's product lines.

Casey is about five feet eleven inches tall and has a clear, light complexion that blends rather unnoticeably into a white shirt. In personality and demeanor, it appears that he would be less at ease at a party than, say, Saranga. Saranga's more extensive contact with upper management has prepared him to converse more freely with a broader section of people. Casey is more comfortable with technical types, such as Hanrahan. But even their styles differ. Hanrahan might boldly walk into a meeting, giving the impression he's the kind of executive who would fight down to the wire for what he believes in. Casey slips quietly into a meeting, with an air of developed confidence that lets you know he knows what he is talking about.

Casey, and Hancock for that matter, are super techies and can look at wild systems diagrams depicting SNA or other complex technology and see more than a bunch of objects tied together by some lines. They not only know that such diagrams depict complex networks of interconnected voice and data products, but they also understand how the technology actually works to make the systems function.

In fact, Hancock and Casey know the two founding fathers of SNA. Dr. Edward Sussenguth, is an IBM Fellow at Research Triangle Park. Paul Lindfors works as a part-time consultant to Mel Deener, head of IBM's U.S.-based briefing centers, and to large SNA customers. Because Sussenguth and Lindfors still work at Research Triangle Park, Casey and Hancock have had ample opportunity to get to know them and to understand why they poured the SNA foundation the way they did.

Dr. Sussenguth went to Raleigh from IBM Kingston in 1971. Shortly thereafter, Paul Lindfors left the Bank of Montreal and joined IBM as Sussenguth's technical assistant. Sussenguth and Lindfors set out to provide a standardized approach for connecting IBM terminals to IBM host computers. Their approach was very different from the one that other developers—Digital Equipment Corporation (DEC) for example—would have followed.

In the early seventies, IBM product managers designed a unique interface for each terminal they wanted to connect with each IBM host computer. N terminals and N host computers led to N times N implementations. That approach wasted research and development money, as well as time. Basically, these developers reinvented part of the wheel each time they developed a unique interface for a product. They also created a rigid set of products that could not easily be changed as IBM added new host computers to its product line. Sussenguth and Lindfors set out to alter that situation.

They developed a standard specification and approach that developers of terminals could use for interconnecting products to the host. This terminal-host interconnect standard provided the foundation for an architected approach to connecting IBM computer/communications network products. Shortly after the development of the specification, IBM designers who wanted their terminals to flow with the mainstream of IBM's computer business adhered to Sussenguth and Lindfors's emerging SNA standard.

Sussenguth and Lindfors's approach helped to establish IBM's three-tiered hierarchical approach for computer/communication networks. This hierarchical approach placed the host or mainframe at the top of the network, as the master controlling nearly everything in the network; the front-end processor (a form of minicomputer) at the next level, aiding the host; and the terminals at the lowest level, serving as slaves. In the basic SNA, depicted in Figure 1, everything was subordinate to the host. Directors of MIS departments, especially those who managed networks that include hosts, minicomputers, and personal computers recognized this hierarchy of computing.

Sussenguth and Lindfors's approach encouraged, if not forced, the trend of concentrating network intelligence—the data that describes the network and routines (or programs) that tell the system what to do—in the host. By the early eighties, IBM expanded SNA's centralized networking capabilities to a well-developed level, controlling probably the most robust centralized approach to networking computers in the industry.

Several years later, other companies began to develop networking using different approaches. DEC began by attacking the problem of transferring files from one computer to another—a peer-to-peer interconnection problem. This led DEC to develop computer/communication network capabilities based on distributing the network intelligence among the computers in the network and not in a central host. In the early 1980s, IBM added peer-to-peer networking capabilities to SNA. Today, SNA offers the benefits of a centralized hierarchical network plus some of the advantages of a decentralized peer-to-peer network.

Knowing how SNA developed helped Hancock and Casey direct the next phase of SNA's development. However, knowing the history of SNA was not enough to understand how to manage that complex communi-

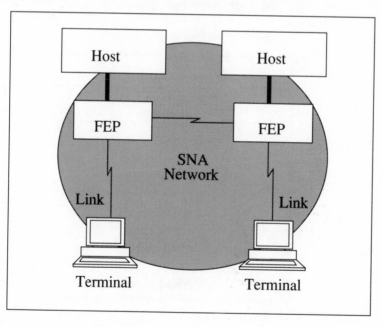

Figure 1 – Basic SNA, 1976

cations technology. Sussenguth and Lindfors's seven-layer SNA model held that key.

Sussenguth and Lindfors had developed a rough model, shown in Figure 2, that could be used to isolate the various functions of a network into one of seven layers, or categories. Isolating the various network functions allows one to focus on a particular aspect of the process. The world standards committee (CCITT) later refined the model to create the OSI Model for interconnecting computer/communication networks.

When asked how the two modest pioneers of SNA discovered the seven-layer model, Sussenguth said that they just sorted networking functions into categories that seemed to make sense at the time. Lindfors added that when they set out to write the first SNA manual,

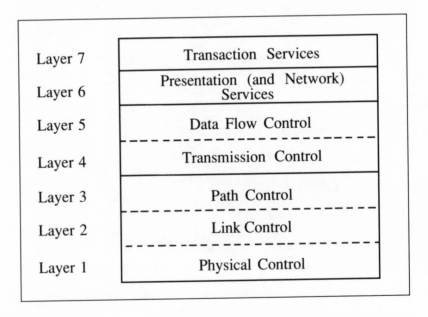

Layer 7	Transaction Services
Layer 6	Presentation (and Network) Services
Layer 5	Data Flow Control
Layer 4	Transmission Control
Layer 3	Path Control
Layer 2	Link Control
Layer 1	Physical Control

Figure 2 – SNA Control Layers

they discovered that eight chapters were needed—one chapter to provide an introduction, and seven more to describe the functioning of the network by category.

Regardless of how the model was developed, Hancock and Casey made good use of it. Without this in-depth knowledge and background in SNA, Casey would never have been asked to join Wheeler's team. And he would never have been asked to attend the Wednesday, February 18 meetings.

7 San Jose, California

Just after the February sun began to peek over the last range of mountains forming the eastern boundary of Silicon Valley and long before the morning breeze blew away the smell of onions that often permeates the Almaden section of Santa Clara Valley, a long black limousine pulled up to the front of Morris Taradalsky's modest San Jose home. Taradalsky, carrying a brown overcoat and wearing a brown suit that matched his hair, quietly took his seat in the back of the vehicle. The limousine drove its lone passenger up the Junipero Serra (Interstate Route 280) to Route 85. Then the chauffeur used 85 to cut across Silicon Valley and link up with Highway 101. They were headed north toward San Francisco Airport for a direct flight to New York's JFK Airport.

Morris Taradalsky is a quiet and contemplative man, reticent about speaking of himself, his accomplishments, or how he fits into the IBM empire.

Walking from the limo into the airport, Taradalsky does not tower over the masses; about five feet eleven inches tall, he inherited his dark complexion from Polish ancestors. If one watches his interaction with people, two characteristics become apparent. First, he treats people politely, nicely. Second, and more interestingly, he resembles Tommy Newsome, Doc Severinson's substitute on Johnny Carson's "Tonight Show." When Johnny tells jokes with Tommy as the butt of them, Tommy always responds by not responding—he silently stares at Johnny with a straight face, deadpanning all comments. Taradalsky's quietness and unwillingness to crack a big smile remind one of the stoic-faced, laconic Tommy.

However, Taradalsky is the butt of no one's jokes. He stands tall in the IBM technical world—so tall that he holds the highest IBM software development position in California, perhaps the highest west of the Rockies and even farther east.

As head of IBM's Santa Teresa Labs, Morris directs an army of 2200 IBM programmers. Although few people outside of IBM recognize the name *Santa Teresa Labs* and perhaps even fewer know the importance it plays in the world software market, STL is by far the world's largest producer of software. STL generates as much revenue as the combined sales of all three giant software companies whose names are practically household words: Ashton-Tate, Microsoft, and Lotus. In 1987, STL generated about $1 billion in sales; Ashton-Tate, Microsoft, and Lotus together produced sales of $1 billion. One reason for STL's anonymity is that its products are sold through other IBM divisions. For simplicity's sake, the name STL is omitted.

Programmers and operators of large 370 systems, however, know STL's products well. Since its creation in 1977, the lab has concentrated primarily on developing software for the 370 MVS operating environment. The thrust of its work has been primarily the development of tools, including (1) computer languages, (2) sorts and merges, and (3) data base management systems.

For example, STL creates the tools that programmers need to develop such applications as reservation systems for airlines and hotels, material requirements planning systems for manufacturers, and customer billing systems for utilities. Some of STL's tools are used only in the development and writing stage of an application; others are embedded in the application program itself and become a part of it. The lab also develops systems software that controls DASD (Direct Access Storage Devices).

On this February morning, Taradalsky faced difficult challenges in two of these areas—computer languages and data base management systems. With respect to languages, there were two nagging issues: (1) COBOL and the OS/2 problem, and (2) development of a language for artificial intelligence applications. These issues concerned several of the people at the next day's meeting, and they would eventually impact even those who knew nothing about them.

Eighty percent of all programs running on IBM glass-house (IBM mainframe computers are usually contained in climate-controlled, secure rooms which are glass on one side) or MVS systems are written in

COBOL, which makes COBOL very important to IBM's prized customers. For that reason, Earl Wheeler and IBM's marketing people wanted COBOL to be on the new OS/2 system. Taradalsky was not exactly in favor of it. Although he had responsibility for developing languages such as FORTRAN, APL, and COBOL; his people don't write code for machines like the PS/2. They write language compilers for the big machines. And there were other reasons: writing language compilers is grunt work, and STL's plate was already full. STL's 2200 programmers were busy; they were not sitting around just waiting for another project. On Wednesday, someone would probably ask, even demand, that Taradalsky resolve this issue.

At the Wednesday morning meeting, he could also expect to be asked for a progress report on the provision of software tools to software companies and users for the development of artificial intelligence applications. Many developers and users were developing primitive AI applications and were clamoring for more IBM software tools. In early 1987, IBM only offered LISP running on VM, PROLOG running on both MVS and VM, and ESE [Expert System Environment—a body of software consisting of a development language and inference (reasoning) engine]. Both LISP and PROLOG were announced as Program Offerings, which means they were not fully supported by IBM. The group at the Wednesday meeting might also question whether STL had the resources to develop all the AI tools in time to support the market's demand.

It was likely that Wheeler would insist that COBOL be supported on the OS/2, and he might demand that these two language issues be resolved before anyone went to the Management Committee meeting in the afternoon. If so, Taradalsky had better have his reply ready.

The data base issue might also emerge at the meeting. The performance characteristics of IMS and DB2 are critical issues to applications developers both inside and outside IBM. Anyone who has stood in a department store and waited more than a few seconds for a computer to check a credit card file before getting a purchase approved, or anyone who has waited on the phone while a ticketing service tries to get computer verification of seating for Saturday night's opera knows the problem. The performance of the computer application is too slow to meet the consumer's level of expectation. The problem lies in systems analysis; the system lacks sufficient communication links, adequate power in the computer hardware and operating system, a sufficiently powerful data base management system, or proper packaging. Although all these components are vital, the DBMS is especially critical to the performance of many applications.

Any discussion about the performance of IMS inevitably leads to dialog about DB2's performance, and vice versa.

IMS processes transactions faster than DB2 does, and there are several reasons why this is so. First, IMS technology has had more time to develop; IMS was announced in 1977, whereas DB2 came out in 1983. IMS developers have had the time to develop unique IMS telecommunication access interfaces, multiple input pipes, on-line recovery features, the facility to add extra processors, and other capabilities to increase performance. Second, the two products apply different data base management technologies. IMS uses a hierarchical, sequential file approach. DB2 is a relational model implementation and stores data in a row–column format. More computer cycles and DASD are required to track data in a relational format. DB2's processing and storage capability needs can bring a 370 VM machine to its knees. DB2 really requires a 370 MVS or 370 MVS/XA (XA stands for Extended Architecture) to run effectively.

IBM promotes IMS for high-performance transaction-based applications such as ATMs (automated teller machines), banking systems, and transportation reservation systems because of its superior performance. It promotes DB2 for use in office automation and management decision support systems. Taradalsky is responsible for seeing that STL's two data bases increase in performance. If *Mr. Performance*, as Taradalsky is known, can accomplish this while improving the performance of IBM's software products, he will have made an important contribution to IBM's success.

IMS's performance has certainly not deteriorated over the past few years. STL has added numerous important features to IMS without slowing the system down. In tomorrow's meeting, he could point out that in 1986, DB2 running on an IBM 30390–200 was benchmarked at 30.9 transactions per second. In 1987, running the same hardware in the same environment, DB2 was clocked at 47.9 transactions per second.

Taradalsky has made other contributions. Back in Poughkeepsie, he had made a name for himself for his work on the MVS operating system. Performance of an operating system determines the performance of a computer system. You can have state-of-the-art hardware, but if the operating system doesn't take full advantage of that hardware, you might as well use an outdated computer. An inadequate operating system gasps as soon as it starts to run a sizable application. That's what causes customers and potential customers to buy from the competition! The MVS had such a performance problem, and Taradalsky improved it in a striking way.

In studying the MVS problem, Taradalsky discovered a way to improve its performance not by 1 or 5%, but by a shocking 25%. Translated into real world measurement, that means that a customer who previously had to purchase a 4Mips (millions of instructions per second) machine to run MVS could now purchase a 3Mips machine and obtain the same performance. A customer who owned a 4Mips machine now had 5Mips performance. For this accomplishment, Taradalsky was one of two developers selected in 1979 to receive a plaque and financial reward for significant contributions to IBM's success.

No doubt Taradalsky had been chosen for Wheeler's team primarily because of his proven abilities in improving the performance of complex software products. He was also on the plane today because IBM needed STL's products. Now, again, it was up to him. As he flew across the country, Taradalsky thought about how he would meet the next day's challenge and how he would handle the questions that might be raised by Wheeler and the other executives.

8   Purchase, New York

FEBRUARY 18, 1987—7:00 A.M.

Earl Wheeler arrived an hour before the meeting. He parked his car in the underground parking lot at the back of IBM's Corporate Staff Headquarters in Purchase, New York. He took the elevator to the third floor, said good morning to a woman working just outside his door, and stepped into the corner office overlooking the rear of the building. He would not reappear until a few minutes before 8 A.M.

By 7:30, the number of cars turning into 2000 Purchase Street had progressed to a near steady flow. Almost all the cars hugged the right side of the headquarters building as they traveled to the rear parking entrance.

This building, with its clean classical lines and long slabs of marble, could easily pass for a museum or national shrine. Designed by world-famous architect I.M. Pei, the award-winning building makes the IBM World

Headquarters building with its afterthought of an atrium look ordinary, a little unplanned, and definitely spartan. Those who have frequented IBM's white, no-frills headquarters or other IBM-owned buildings around the world might wonder why the 1,200 people in this building rate this expense. The building had been originally designed as corporate headquarters for Nestlé–U.S. During construction, Nestlé experienced staffing cutbacks, and the building, with minor remodeling, was sold to IBM. In 1983, several IBM corporate staff departments became its first occupants.

A few cars containing Wheeler's guests began to arrive at the Purchase entrance. One was driven by Peter Dance, a high-ranking executive from IBM's sales and marketing organization, the Information System Group (ISG).

Marketing

Earlier that morning, Peter Dance—Group Director of Software Management, the same business unit that Mike Saranga reports to—had pulled out of the circular driveway in front of his light blue Connecticut home. Like Saranga, he exited the Hutchinson Parkway, made a quick right and then a short left into the IBM Corporate Staff Headquarters.

Dance, head software marketer, already had an opportunity that many marketing executives envied. IBM planners expected the company's software revenues to grow from roughly 10% of IBM's 1987 revenues to perhaps 30% of its 1990 revenues. This was not only possible but highly desirable. If the planners' estimates were correct, this tall, dapper Kentuckian was well positioned to work a growing market *and* to play in a game that was eagerly watched by the top brass of IBM. Dozens of IBM marketing managers wished they had that opportunity.

Dance knew that the 8 A.M. meeting could provide him with the focus and resources he needed to succeed at his job. He knew that Wheeler had put a powerful team together. The four development VPs were practicing a wedge block. If they all blocked together, a huge hole would open. The pigskin would be tossed to Dance, and he would dart through the hole. Who knew how far he'd get?

Dance thinks in terms of football more than most people. He's possibly the Fighting Irish's most avid fan, at least in Connecticut, possibly New England. Notre Dame memorabilia decorate his office. He is also more punctual than most people. Not wanting to miss the opening kickoff, Dance arrived at the Purchase Corporate building more than half an hour early.

Dance had visited this IBM location before, perhaps as many as a dozen times, to meet with Mitchell Watson, Corporate Vice President of Marketing, or his staff. Dance worked with the Corporate Marketing people to establish how his department could best provide marketing support for the software products of various IBM divisions. As 1986 ended, these meetings increasingly focused on Earl Wheeler's project. Dance suspected that Wheeler's project would some day be called the Super-Super Bowl of Computing—and that before it was, it would require a marketing thrust that encompassed the entire company.

During some of these visits to Purchase, Dance had met with Earl Wheeler and/or his staff. Because of his position and expertise, Dance had been selected to share the company's "combined marketing wisdom" with Wheeler and his four all-pro linemen. Wheeler meets a dozen or so $100-million-a-year customers annually. Saranga, Casey, Hanrahan, and Taradalsky occasionally meet with customers to discuss their requirements and to explain IBM's R&D direction; but none of the four is as close to the market as those who work it every day. That's why they needed Dance.

Every company has a combined marketing wisdom, a consensus that encompasses the reality of the situation in the marketplace and what should be done. IBM is no different in that respect. If anything, because IBM applies good communication practices, it seems to form a consensus better than most companies, but that does not mean that its consensus is always correct.

The judgment of the IBM sales and marketing people in early February appeared to be that the slowing growth of the computer industry, which over the last few years had dropped from double-digit to single-digit growth, had been largely caused by hardware and software vendors like themselves. Dance and his marketing colleagues believed that companies like IBM had introduced such a proliferation of new and difficult-to-use technology that customers needed time to assimilate the computer/communications products they had before they again went on a buying spree.

Communicating with Computers

As Dance and the IBM marketing organization saw it, users have a difficult time communicating with the computers (terminals, PCs, and workstations). The keyboard, prompts, procedures, and everything else a user experiences when he or she uses a computer is called the user/computer access interface. Unfortunately, few people have an innate ability to use a keyboard, know what procedures they must follow, or know how to respond to cryptic prompts to get a dumb terminal, a PC, or a high-performance workstation to do something for them. Steve Wozniak of Apple and Bill Gates of Microsoft may be the exceptions. Not only was it well accepted that users have trouble learning to use the present generation of user/computer interfaces, Dance and his marketing associates knew that IBM exacerbated this problem.

Consider just the keyboard issue for a moment. IBM provides customers with several different types of keyboards. Whenever someone uses a keyboard that differs from one that he or she had used previously, productivity goes to pot until the user becomes familiar with the new layout of the keys. Consider a user of an IBM PC who switches to an IBM 3270 terminal. The difference in the placement of keys is so great that the user must relearn where everything is.

IBM is not the only company to be blamed for offering uncommon keyboards. Apple Computer's IIe keyboard differs from that of the Macintosh. DEC and HP are just as much at fault. Almost all computer vendors support multiple keyboards, and users have difficulty in switching from one keyboard to another. Users as a group waste hundreds of thousands of hours learning or relearning how to use one of the many keyboards out there and to correct the mistake of an uneducated finger.

Consider another aspect of interfacing with a terminal, PC, or workstation. Besides nonstandard keyboards there is no common way in which the prompts on the displays present and request information. Anyone who has used more than one software program knows the problem.

In the first place, it takes too long to master any software package. It takes days, even weeks, of usage to master half the features of, for example, a word processing package. Moreover, for some reason—and there often is reason—you may want to switch from one application program to another. For example, you might want to switch from Microsoft® Word to MicroPro's Word-Star™. Or you may want to switch from one of the popular PC-based desktop publishing systems such as Aldus's PageMaker® or Xerox®'s Ventura Publisher to a desktop publishing system like Frame Technology's Frame Maker™ that runs on high-performance workstations. Mastering the new program takes a great deal of time even though you already are familiar with the operations of the same generic type of software. The reason for this? Every software developer has laid out the screen and the prompts differently. That means you have to learn a new system. That means users can't easily transfer what they have already learned.

Inconsistent Programming Tools

Dance and the IBM marketers recognized another problem. The world is not made up of "ultimate users." Hundreds of thousands of programmers work daily with computers. They too have a problem interfacing with the tools of their trade.

Anyone who has programmed computers, especially in a multisystem environment, appreciates how difficult it is to work without a consistent set of programming tools. Consider the problem of a company that has an application that requires System/36 as well as System/370 class machines. The programmers use the RPG language to write a program for the System/36, but then use COBOL or other mainline 370 languages for the System/370. This creates a huge problem for Mr. Good Code. He had just learned how to use one set of tools; now he has to learn to use another set of tools. If the software tools on both families were consistent, he could start work on the 370 task immediately after he completed the /36 program.

Or consider a large IBM customer that may have invested heavily in training 30 or 40 programmers to use 370-based tools effectively to build parts of distributed or cooperative processing applications. That customer may now want to disperse 3Xs and/or PCs into the system. The customer can't just plug 3Xs and PCs into the wall and have the enterprisewide system work—programmers must write some code to meet that firm's specific needs. Since the 3X and PC have their own set of programming tools and since it is unlikely that the 30 or 40 System/370 programmers have any skill in using 3X or PC tools (at best, one can hope they are a bit rusty), the customer must either invest in retraining programmers or hire another crop of them. Neither solution is desirable and both contribute to delays in implementing technology. Again the problem is lack of consistent tools across disparate hardware environments.

Dance, representing the combined wisdom of IBM, would not want to spend time explaining how IBM came to offer three sets of inconsistent software tools. He would agree that a common set of programming tools would greatly simplify the work of programmers, especially those who communicate with multiple systems. The availability of common software tools across the three IBM hardware families would enable the customers to save billions of dollars in programming costs and to get things done much sooner.

Lack of Communications Support

Dance knew that the ultimate users and programmers are not the only ones who have a difficult time communicating with computers. Systems analysts also have a problem. They have difficulty in making computers communicate with each other—interconnecting computers is no easy game.

For example, if you took all the communications functions of one computer and sorted them into Sussenguth and Lindfors's seven layers of SNA, you would have a profile of the communications characteristics of one of those systems. If you did the same for each of the other two systems, you would have the communication characteristics of all three systems. The three profiles would not be identical. No one would expect that the designers of the PC family in Boca Raton, the midrange designer of the System/36 and System/38, or the mainframe designers of the various 370 models would or could design their systems with the same communications profile.

Over the last five years, IBM and other computer and communications companies have inundated information systems (IS) managers with new technology. In 1986, IBM first announced a broadband local area networking scheme, later a baseband local area networking system, and then enhancements to ROLM's CBX. All offered customers different approaches to interconnect data and/or voice products. However, because of the complexity of the customers' requirements and the technology proposed as a solution, it could take a customer a year to figure out which approach or approaches to take. It could take even longer to implement the solution.

Ellen Hancock and Don Casey claim to be providing a solution to the growing communications problem. Many of the extensions and enhancements to SNA in the last few years have made possible the interworking of all three of IBM's computer families—370, 3X, and PC. But this attempt to develop a common communications solution lacked the breadth that a full solution across all product lines could provide.

Developing Portable Applications

IBM's top marketing managers wanted Dance to help the developers appreciate the importance of the lack of portable application programs. This problem hurt customers and kept IBM from scoring a lot of touchdowns.

Anyone who has invested in an application program and wants to move that program onto a newer, faster, or in some other way more desirable computer appreciates the problem of lack of portability. That person is locked in, and it's expensive to get unlocked. Consider, for example, a small or medium-sized manufacturer running MAPICS (manufacturing accounting production information and control system) application software on a top-of-the-line System/36 that can no longer handle the increased requirements placed on it because the company's business has expanded or use of the System/36 has become more pervasive. It's okay when IBM tells the customer it needs some new hardware. It's okay because most people philosophically accept that when their requirements expand beyond the scope of their current hardware, they will have to purchase new equipment. But then the customer says: "Okay, how much is the next size System/36 processor?"

It's less okay when Dance or his colleagues say: "IBM does not offer a larger System/36 processor—the system was not designed to be expanded. You need to switch up to the 370 family, you need to start using 370 processors."

At this point, the average System/36 customer would start to reach for the red flag; but the real trouble would start when the customer learned it would need to replace all the System/36 terminals. System/36 terminals don't work with the System/370—you need 3270 terminals.

In addition, the customer's System/36 application program—MAPICS—does not run in the 370 environment; the 370 runs COPICS (Communications Oriented Production and Information Control System). The functional difference between MAPICS and COPICS is similar in scope to the difference between the cockpit of a Boeing 707 and a Lockheed L1011. Not only will the customer have to make a hardware change, he will lose the thousands of dollars he invested training everyone to operate and use MAPICS, and he will lose the special reports he has written.

IBM has been thrown out of the game a lot in the mid-eighties because of the company's inability to port software across IBM product lines. And as soon as DEC learns that IBM has been thrown out of a game, it quickly suits up and promises the customer that it will never act that way. The inability to migrate application software across IBM families of computers has cost the company a few billions in sales.

Who's to Blame?

Neither Dance nor the rest of the IBM marketing organization would blame Casey, Hanrahan, Taradalsky, and Saranga—four of the company's top developers—for all the difficulty the ultimate users, programmers, and systems analysts faced utilizing computer products. Nor would they make light of the subject.

The current problem is reminiscent of that in the 1960s when IBM defied the principles that helped it first to obtain dominance of the computer industry and succeed with the System/360. IBM violated the principle that states: Thou shalt protect thy customers' investment in an application by enabling the customer to migrate that application to more powerful hardware as needed. IBM failed to provide one class of customers—users of the System/36—with a migration path to a more powerful hardware that would protect their investment. Dance had been invited to this morning's meeting to make sure that all four developers appreciated the significance of this problem and recognized just how important it was to find a solution.

Kickoff in Five

Dance, Saranga, Hanrahan, and Taradalsky had gathered in the cafeteria. Ever-punctual, Dance rechecked his watch—kickoff in five minutes. All of them repressed their excitement. In five minutes, Saranga, Hanrahan, Taradalsky, and Casey, four of the most competent development executives in the world who represented the resources of four separate IBM divisions, would review their attack plans with Earl Wheeler and tie up any loose ends before driving to the MC meeting in Armonk. In five minutes, they would have to assure Wheeler that they and their teams were fully committed to launch the plan that would provide users and developers with the means to slash the time and cost of implementing and using IBM computer products—the means that would enable IBM to attain a new level of dominance in the world computer market.   235738.

The last minutes ticked away. The conversation turned to Casey—no one had seen him. Dance and Saranga both had operations in the Raleigh area and knew it had been hit by a storm. No one asked what would happen if the glue man didn't show.

9 Band–Aid, Break-through, or Enchilada?

While Dance and the three development executives—Hanrahan, Saranga, and Taradalsky—exchanged conversation and mild concern over Casey's whereabouts, a long black Coach Limousine pulled up to the front door. A man jumped out, paid the driver, and then ran past the 36-foot-wide beech tree to the left of the Purchase building's front entrance. At the reception desk, a women inquired whether he was an IBM employee or a guest. He immediately answered. She politely pointed to the IBM Employee Guest Book and asked him to sign in before taking the elevator upstairs.

John Friedline, slightly out of breath, stepped out of the third floor elevator and made his way toward the group standing on the fringe of the cafeteria area. Peter Dance was especially relieved to see his assistant. The

101

slides Dance needed for today's meetings were in Friedline's dark brown briefcase.

A check of the records of the Tarrytown, New York,
Marriott Hotel would show that Friedline, as well as
George Liptak, had checked in roughly one week ago.
They came from IBM's Atlanta, Georgia, offices. Liptak
had checked out this morning, but Friedline had not.

Both Friedline and Liptak have extensive marketing
experience. Each, at separate times, has held the position of Manager of IBM's Office Systems and thus, thoroughly understands IBM's office products and the
needs of that market. Friedline also had experience marketing the System/36 as well as IBM's high-performance workstation, the RT PC. Liptak also had a lot of
experience marketing everything from word processing
systems to small business computers. Both men have
extremely creative minds—they expertly take abstrac-
tions and develop good marketing concepts. Because of
those skills, they were selected to help Dance prepare
his presentation for Wheeler's 8:00 A.M. meeting, the
afternoon MC meeting, and whatever was expected to
transpire after that meeting.

Breakthrough or Band–Aid

What were the development VP's working on that
could be so important that two marketing executives
were needed to fly in for a week to help a third marketing executive prepare a short speech? What could the
developers do that would rate as a *breakthrough*? What
could they do to solve the problems facing customers?

Well, they could do many things to make it easier and less costly for customers to implement computer products. However, to do something on the level of a breakthrough, a real breakthrough, they would have to do something significant in each of the four problem areas of computing. They would have to (1) clean up the user access mess—eliminate or reduce dissimilar or uncommon keyboards, and develop a more consistent way for users to communicate with computers; (2) provide programmers with a set of consistent programming tools; (3) provide systems analysts and programmers with a consistent set of communications support for applications that makes it easier to interface with programs; and (4) create an environment where users could migrate application programs from one IBM hardware environment to another. They would have to hit all four at once for a breakthrough. Overcoming the difficulties in one area helps, but since all aspects are inter-related, improvements are needed in each area.

A real breakthrough would be some product equal in magnitude to the System/360 or SNA, something that would significantly slash the time and cost of developing meaningful applications and that would save users time.

Friedline's briefcase contained a diagram like that shown in Figure 1, with blocks labeled *Common User Access*, *Common Programming Interface*, *Application Enabling Products*, *Common Communication's Support* and three blocks labeled with the names of IBM's three hardware families.

Some people at IBM were at least thinking about the four different aspects of computing. They were thinking about those four aspects of computing across the PC, 3X, and 370 product lines. And the fact that four development executives, one for each of the problem areas, had been invited to today's meeting added credibility to the idea that IBM might be going for the whole enchilada rather than a Band–Aid. But applying something of this magnitude to the multi-billion dollar software effort would take incredible cooperation among four strong-willed individualists and a complete change of IBM's thinking. It would make more sense to assume that IBM was attacking a less grandiose problem or just Band–Aiding one. But it wasn't.

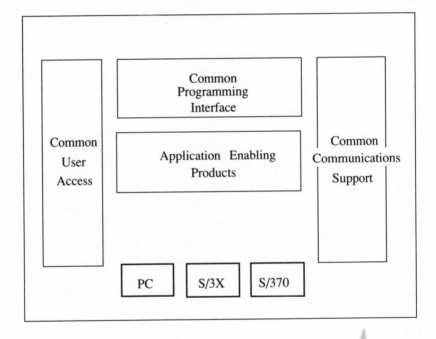

Figure 1 – Diagram in Friedline's Briefcase

Systems Application Architecture

A few months ago, this project had become important enough for IBM to give it a name. IBM's formal Naming Committee considered hundreds of possible selections before settling on the jargon-rich nomenclature—Systems Application Architecture—that made even the high priests of computerdom scratch their heads.

The committee attempted to capture, in as few words as possible, the essence of what this team was developing. The words *systems* and *architecture* fit well. Wheeler and the four development executives were developing a *system*—a coordinated body of methods and machines—and an *architecture*—an organized assemblage of things or parts that form a complex whole. The word *application* was also appropriate, for the primary purpose of the system and architecture was to facilitate the use and propagation of application programs. Systems Application Architecture, better than any other term, expressed the essence of the project.

At 8 A.M., the gathered team members waited to walk the path to Wheeler's conference room. Allan Atherton—Technical Assistant to Earl Wheeler—appeared from the closed doors near Wheeler's office. For someone who is in daily contact with a man known as the 800-pound gorilla, he did not look any the worse for wear.

When the executives entered the conference room, their mild concerns for Casey's whereabouts ended. They spotted Don Casey in the back of the room, rearranging his overheads. He had apparently arrived early, grabbed a cup of coffee, and headed directly for the conference room. Since none of the other participants knew the extent of the storm, none thought to ask how in the world he got out of Raleigh. If they had, Casey would have reassured them that he had left a few days before the storm hit for a marketing conference in Fort Lauderdale, Florida. He left on Sunday, one day before the ice started to fall, and on Tuesday afternoon caught an Eastern Airline flight to La Guardia. Not to worry!

While the group settled in and awaited Wheeler, Al Atherton placed a telephone call to Armonk—an anxious AA needed to be assured that Casey was in attendance.

10 Wheeler Recruits Hanrahan

PURCHASE, NEW YORK

Earl Wheeler and Dick Hanrahan had their first private one-on-one in Wheeler's office in early 1986. At that time, Hanrahan was being considered for the position of Vice President of Programming for the Entry Systems Division. Bill Lowe, President of ESD, asked Wheeler to assist in assessing Hanrahan's capabilities. Wheeler obliged. If Lowe had not asked, Wheeler would have insisted that he be allowed to check Hanrahan out—for a good reason. The person selected would have to meet Earl Wheeler's requirements as well as Bill Lowe's.

Bill Lowe had one very clearly defined objective for the VP of Programming: get the PS/2 software—which is 95% of the division's PS/2 product—designed, tested, and out the door as soon as humanly possible.

IBM recognized that its big mainframe customer base would, for as long as anyone could see, provide a steady stream of revenue. That part of the business would be like that of the seven regional Bell companies—a guaranteed source of revenue and profits. However, IBM could no longer count on the mainframe side of the business for extensive growth. The growth opportunities now lay, to a large extent, in personal computers or workstations. Bill Lowe had to push the PS/2 into the marketplace as soon as possible. Otherwise, the window of opportunity would disappear.

For this ambitious project, Lowe needed a leader like General George Patton. He needed a tough, tenacious development executive who would attack relentlessly, and then attack again—someone who would smash, shake up, or do whatever else was needed to solve any problems that hindered the development of the PS/2 software. The basic software would consist of the Microsoft–developed OS/2 operating system; the extended version would include a data base management system called the Data Manager, and a set of programs aptly named the Communication Manager, which would enable the PS/2 to communicate with other computers. It also would include software—the Presentation Manager—to facilitate communication between the user and the PS/2. The sooner the extended version of the software became available, the sooner Lowe could expect PS/2 sales to skyrocket. And the sooner IBM's MC would know whether the company had seized that huge window of opportunity.

Earl Wheeler, too, recognized that the development of the PS/2 was an unprecedented opportunity—and not just for personal computers. IBM forecasters expected to sell about 10,000 PS/2s daily by early 1988. Aside from creating great profits for IBM, sales of this magnitude would create a huge base of PS/2 users. That base could ensure the success of several aspects of Wheeler's Systems Application Architecture strategy. To achieve that objective, Wheeler, too, needed someone with Patton's qualities.

Common User Interface

A large base of PS/2 users could be the catalyst for fulfilling Wheeler's dream of a common user access interface. If millions of people bought and used PS/2s, a large installed base of users would be familiar with the user access interface of one computer. If Wheeler could then convince developers of the 3X follow-on product and the 370 terminals/workstations to incorporate the same user access as that of the PS/2 in their designs, common user access would be implemented across the three hardware environments.

Cooperative Processing

The PS/2 could also be used to create an environment for cooperative processing on enterprise-wide computing systems. Large numbers of installed PS/2s create a need for interconnection. However, for practical and meaningful interconnection of workstations, the data base management systems, interfaces to those DBMS, and communication technology of the PS/2 must be consistent.

To this end, Wheeler wanted the user access interface for the PS/2—the Presentation Manager—to be designed in such a way that it would be relatively easy to get the builders of the 3X follow-on and the 370 terminals/workstations to incorporate the Presentation Manager into their future products. Also, he wanted to ensure that the PS/2's Data Manager, the programmer interface to the Data Manager, and the Communication Manager would create an environment conducive to interconnectivity and cooperative processing. Getting the right person as VP of Programming was crucial to the success of this strategy.

Wheeler Sizes Up Hanrahan

Hanrahan's first visit to Wheeler's office was a let's-get-to-know-each-other session. Wheeler already knew a lot about Hanrahan. The question was: Can he handle the scope of this project, and is he flexible enough to make a switch from a large system orientation to the PS/2 and common user access?

They discussed a lot of issues. Wheeler told Hanrahan that, in 1984, the Management Committee had decided to put a team together to develop a multifunction operating system. Multifunction means different things in different settings. Wheeler's frame of reference had to do with operating system functions. An operating system like PC-DOS the one that controls the original IBM PC has limited functionality. It controls the basic function of the computer, and that's it. A multifunction operating system, on the other hand, would offer more, such as data base management capability and communication management functions. The operating system for the OS/2 would have a built-in DBMS and data communications manager.

Wheeler explained that the purpose of the multifunction operating system was essentially to help forge a tight relationship between families of products—for example, the PS/2 and 370. He stressed these products because he was trying to make a point about the advancement of PS/2 technology and the need to integrate that technology with the 370 technology. Also, he was talking to someone who had 20 years of 370 experience. If he'd been talking with someone with an equal amount of experience in the midrange area, he might have stressed the need to integrate the 370 and the System/36 or System/38 technologies.

Wheeler went on to say that workstation technology is advancing at 20% to 25% percent annually. He expected the PS/2 or workstation technology to advance so rapidly within the next few years that the dumb terminals now in front of the 370 would soon advance to PS/2 status. It was only a question of time before products like the PS/2 Model 80 were connected to mainframes. With that, Wheeler paused and waited for Hanrahan's reaction.

Hanrahan nodded in agreement. The sooner IBM provided terminals with the power of some of today's high-performance workstations, the better, in his view.

Wheeler's blue eyes sparkled. He sensed that Hanrahan appreciated the importance of the advancing workstation technology. Some people who had grown up with the 370 technology saw more 370 processor power and storage capability as the only solution to problems.

Bob Markell, the VP of Programming whose job Hanrahan was being considered for, had worked to help forge a tighter relationship between users of 370 terminals and the PS/2 product line. Wheeler asked Hanrahan what he thought about that topic.

Hanrahan, too, believed that IBM needed to provide users with seamless solutions. He went to great length to emphasize the importance of the PS/2 technology, the need to forge relationships between the PS/2 and the 370, and the need to get the job done now.

At some point, it became apparent to Wheeler that Hanrahan might be the leader he and Lowe needed. The remaining question was: Did Hanrahan appreciate the importance of the common user interface, and would he agree to work closely with him to make it a reality?

Cementing Relationships

Wheeler told Hanrahan that a consistent user interface would be needed to cement a real relationship between the PS/2 and the future workstations that would hang on the 370. The big hole in IBM's product line was the lack of a consistent user interface. In many cases, IBM had consistency by product, but rarely by system. Development of the interface was paramount. It would be optimized for the workstation of the future and would run primarily on PS/2 and OS/2 technologies.

Hanrahan grasped Wheeler's big picture, but wanted more specifics about the scope of the common user interface—he hadn't heard about any development plan.

Wheeler explained that considerable work had gone into developing the concepts for the common user interface. Common user access defines the rules for the dialog between the human and the computer. It establishes how information appears on a display screen and how people respond to that information. It includes definitions of interface elements and rules for interaction techniques such as panel appearance, procedures for moving from one panel to another, function selection, color and emphasis, help messages, and terminology.

Hanrahan said he understood.

Then Wheeler opened a manila folder and placed on the overhead projector a slide that looked somewhat like Figure 1.

He said that the elements of the interface would offer physical, syntactical, and semantic consistency across much of the product line from the PS/2 to 370. A slide that looked very much like Figure 2 dealt with examples of physical consistency.

Then Wheeler placed two more slides (Figures 3 and 4) on the projector, giving Hanrahan time to read the

```
+------------------------------------------------+
|                                                |
|       ◆       Physical  Consistency            |
|                                                |
|       ◆       Syntactical  Consistency         |
|                                                |
|       ◆       Semantic  Consistency            |
|                                                |
|    PS/2 <------------------------>370          |
+------------------------------------------------+
```

Figure 1 – Elements of an Interface

Physical consistency refers to hardware: the keyboard
layout, the location of keys, and the use of the mouse,
For example, it would be physically consistent for the
function keys to be in the same place on the keyboard
regardless of system. Likewise, it would be physically
consistent always to use button 1 on a mouse to
select an item.

PS/2 <————————————————>370

Figure 2 – Physical Inconsistency

Syntactical consistency refers to the sequence and
order in which elements appear on the display screen
(the presentation language) and the sequence of
keystrokes to request action (the actual language).
For example, it would be syntactically consistent to
always center the panel title at the top of the panel.

PS/2 <————————————————>370

Figure 3 – Syntactical Consistency

Semantic consistency refers to the meaning of the
elements that make up the interface. For example,
it would be semantically consistent for the command
CANCEL to have the same meaning (where the
command takes users and what happens next) on
all systems.

PS/2 <————————————————>370

Figure 4 – Semantic Consistency

words and grasp the meaning of syntactical consistency and semantic consistency—two important concepts.

Hanrahan thought that it would be a great idea to develop a consistent user interface across the IBM hardware lines. It would eliminate or at least minimize dissimilar keyboards and create a more unified approach to screen layouts and prompts.

Wheeler nodded and confided that the Management Committee had agreed that the Presentation Manager of the PS/2 needed to be driven across the 3X and the 370 line.

Wheeler continued: "The Presentation Manager being developed for the PS/2 defines how users communicate with the PS/2 and vice versa. Whoever is selected as the VP of Programming will have to help create the common user access, not just produce a Presentation Manager. And then there is also the larger importance of developing the Data Manager and the interfaces for it."

After nearly two hours had passed, Dick Hanrahan left the meeting. Shortly thereafter, he got the job.

Snowed Under

Before being asked by Wheeler to prepare for the February 18 meeting, Hanrahan had made a major commitment to his boss, Bill Lowe, and to the Management Committtee to announce the PS/2 on April 2. Before IBM could make that announcement, software plans for the PS/2 and the basic version of the OS/2 had to be reviewed. Announcement literature had to be prepared and double-checked. Hanrahan had dozens of meetings with his staff, the marketing staff, and others to work out the details. These tasks, on top of his regular work, would consume much of his time.

When Wheeler called Hanrahan to solicit his help on the SAA announcement, Hanrahan explained that he had previously signed up for the April 2 PS/2 announcement, but that his role in that effort would pretty much end about a week before the announcement. At that point, he might have some available time.

Wheeler said he needed Hanrahan immediately— regardless of other commitments—*the SAA announcement might precede the PS/2 announcement.*

"Impossible!" Hanrahan replied.

Wheeler argued that much of the preparation for the SAA announcement could be used for the PS/2 announcement.

Hanrahan answered: "Yes and no."

Wheeler asserted: "Find a way. Everyone is counting on you. We need your help. The final checkoff date for planning the announcement is February 18. Morris, Mike, and Don have agreed they can make it. Dance says he can make it. That leaves you. Think about it and call me back."

Hanrahan had little choice but to make the commitment. Wheeler didn't make frivolous requests. And Wheeler had hit his hot button—yes, he could get the job done. He would find a way to accomplish his regular day-to-day work, or at least what really had to get done. He would continue to prepare for the PS/2 announcement. And somehow he would immediately start pulling SAA material together as well.

11   Hanrahan Makes His Pitch

FEBRUARY 18, 1987—8 A.M.

Earl Wheeler, taller and older than any of the four development executives, left his corner office and headed down the hall to the conference room. There he warmly greeted his guests. Each man then took his seat. All knew exactly why they were there—to see that they had their act together before they attended the Management Committee meeting later in the afternoon.

Wheeler and his guests—the four development executives (Hanrahan, Casey, Saranga, and Taradalsky), the marketing executives (Dance and Friedline), and some assistants—were meeting this morning to discuss the

117

next step of SAA, the project that would give customers what they needed. The executives in this conference room planned to attack not one piece of the problem of using computer products, but all four problem areas of computing:

- How users communicate with computers

- How programmers interact with computers

- How computers communicate with other computers

- The lack of application programs, especially portable applications

They were addressing all the major problems in the grandiose plan they called the Systems Application Architecture (SAA) strategy.

Some people outside IBM believe this project will take as long to mature as SNA took—roughly 10 years—although IBM strongly disagrees with this projection. Some competitors might say it is no more than a marketing ploy. Others will say that it is so complex that it is not understandable. Some will grumble that no competitor has the resources to counter it. Others will assert that SAA will motivate unlikely couples— such as Apple and DEC, and AT&T and Sun Microsystems—to work together.

Undaunted by criticisms and detractors, present or future, Wheeler fully expected the four development executives and Dance to demonstrate today that each one of them was fully prepared to publicly launch SAA. If they were not ready. . . !

Wheeler opened this final prelaunch session by asking Dick Hanrahan to be the first presenter. That suggestion sat well with Hanrahan. If he got it over with now, he could sit back and relax. He might even enjoy the rest of the meeting.

Hanrahan stood and walked to the overhead projector on the far end of the conference table. His face showed signs of fatigue. He began by stating that he would briefly review the status of the main component of the common user access—the Presentation Manager. Then he would report on the Data Manager and the Communication Manager. He told the group that if they had questions, they should ask them as he went along.

Presentation Manager

Hanrahan told the group that he had a commitment from the product manager that the Presentation Manager would be available before the end of 1988, possibly even by October, and that the product would meet all the technical requirements to be a part of SAA.

A tentative smile appeared on Wheeler's face. In less than two years, he, IBM, the customers, and the rest of the industry would have the decisive software product needed to make common user access a reality. The Presentation Manager was the cornerstone of Wheeler's plan to create a common user access. Without it he had, at best, some good ideas that might never materialize.

No one in this group was surprised to hear that the Presentation Manager would not be available until late 1988, even though they all knew that everyone in the Entry Systems Division and in other IBM groups wanted it out as soon as possible.

IBM believed that the availability of the PS/2 even without the Presentation Manager would still attract the attention of software companies that had already developed software for IBM's PC-DOS personal computers. A lot of those companies would shift from marketing their IBM PC software to the newer PS/2 line. What IBM really wanted was for software companies already providing IBM PC–based software to start writing new applications that would open new markets for the PS/2. They also wanted the software companies that were writing for competitors' machines, such as Apple on the low end and Sun Microsystems on the higher end of the technology spectrum, to write software for the IBM PS/2. For any of this to happen, however, the software developers needed the Presentation Manager.

Entry Systems Division also wanted the Presentation Manager available as soon as possible to eliminate what might be Apple's only technological advantage over IBM: communication between the user and the Apple Macintosh was superior to that between the user and the PC or the PS/2 without the Presentation Manager.

Wheeler asked: "Are you really sure that the Presentation Manager will be available no later than 1988?"

Hanrahan replied that he had just returned from another trip to Hursley, England, for a firsthand, up-to-date report on the status of the Presentation Manager. The greatest concentration of IBM programmers with expertise in the development of text and graphic display software was in IBM's U.K. labs; therefore, the bulk of the work for the Presentation Manager was being done there. The English were incorporating U.S. windowing advancements with existing 370 display software. The product would be ready.

Data Manager

Satisfied with Hanrahan's response, Wheeler asked him to report on the commitment or lack of commitment for the Data Manager. As he said that, he looked first at Hanrahan and then at Taradalsky, both of whom interpreted the gesture to mean that both of them might have to contribute to answering the question. Both were involved with the Data Manager.

Hanrahan's people in Austin, Texas, who were responsible for developing the Data Manager for the PS/2, were applying a relational model to develop the data base. However, most of IBM's relational data base technology resided in Taradalsky's Santa Teresa Labs. Wheeler had insisted that Taradalsky loan several of his people experienced in relational data base technology to the Austin team.

Hanrahan smiled and told Wheeler that the Data Manager also would be available in late 1988. His programmers, with the help of some of Taradalsky's people, had things under control. Enough progress had been made that many of the Santa Teresa people were already on their way home.

"What about the programmer interface that needs to be built onto the front end of the Data Manager?" Wheeler queried. Hanrahan paused for a moment, but then Wheeler quickly withdrew his question. That was Taradalsky's responsibility.

Communication Manager

Wheeler asked about the progress of the Communication Manager—part of the extended version of the OS/2, which was also being developed in Austin, Texas.

Hanrahan said that the product manager of the Communication Manager had committed to conform to Casey's SAA communication support requirement. Wheeler quickly looked at Casey. Hanrahan did the same. Casey, apparently thinking about something else, looked surprised. Hanrahan repeated the statement. Casey, embarrassed, nodded his head in agreement. Saranga chuckled quietly.

Continuing, Hanrahan stated that Austin would add LU6.2 hooks and calls (software that "hooks" on to other software and "calls" other programs) into the Communication Manager so that PS/2s with the extended version of the OS/2 could effectively communicate with all other products that conform to SAA requirements. He expected the Communication Manager to be available in July 1988.

Earl Wheeler must have breathed a sigh of relief—one down, three to go. He pretty much had his common user interface. Hanrahan had done it; he had succeeded in obtaining commitments to conform to SAA requirements from the product managers of the Presentation Manager, the Data Manager, the Communication Manager, and the manager of the overall OS/2 development. And it looked as if the products would get out well within two years from the announcement date.

Wheeler thought that they might be able to

announce the SAA in 30 days—3 months, worst case. Regardless, Hanrahan's products would meet the time requirement. Now, if only Taradalsky, Casey, and Saranga could deliver.

12 Wheeler's Task Forces

FEBRUARY 18, 1987—8:44 A.M.

Dick Hanrahan slumped in his chair; Morris Taradalsky sat at attention.

Wheeler, fixing his eyes on Taradalsky, asked if he had obtained commitments from all nine software product managers whose products would be part of the initial SAA offering. Wheeler knew that Taradalsky had already landed most of the key product managers. However, he did not know the status of the others.

Product managers who couldn't or wouldn't agree to meet the SAA programming interface specifications would have their products omitted from the initial SAA announcement. If any of the key product managers backed out, God help them. If too few managers signed up, the SAA announcement would have to be delayed.

Taradalsky was accountable for attaining the product managers' acceptance and for providing this information at this morning's meeting. He thought back to the road he'd traveled over the last year and recalled just how he'd taken on this responsibility.

Wheeler Taps Taradalsky

About a year ago, Taradalsky had received a polite invitation to visit Wheeler. Taradalsky, a division Vice President and development executive in another organization, could have refused the invitation, but respect, consideration, inquisitiveness, and downright good political sense dictated that when the corporation's highest ranking software executive beckons, you go.

At that first meeting Wheeler unveiled his plan to create a new computing environment and outlined the scope of the project—the creation of four levels of consistency: user access, communications, programming, and applications across disparate environments.

Taradalsky was taken aback. Creating consistent application enabling software just across the 370 product line was a tremendous problem, one that Wheeler had been trying to solve since 1980. Much of the progress that had been made was at the operating system and communications software levels. At the application enabling layer, many software products were still not consistent across the 370 operating environments. So Taradalsky was understandably surprised when Wheeler told him the time had come to make an all-out effort to create a set of consistent application enabling software not only across the 370 environment, but also encompassing the 3X and the PC.

Taradalsky thought the idea a good one. Consistent software across the 370 product line alone offered plenty of benefits. If his own 2200 programmers had consistent software tools for the 370 product line, he would see a significant increase in their productivity. This increase would help him meet the financial objectives he had committed to attain. Billings to other divisions would increase, and costs would be held in check.

A consistent set of 370 software would solve several other annoying problems. As the corporation continued to place greater demands on the Santa Teresa Labs, Taradalsky's army of programmers kept growing. It already overflowed the STL complex, and Armonk had denied them permission to build another wing onto the complex. The overflow had to be housed in IBM's Menlo Park, California, offices. This created major inefficiencies and morale problems. Consistent 370 software would enable the existing programmers to meet increasing demands, obviating the need to add more people and thus easing the housing problem.

The Systems Product Division in Rochester, Minnesota, which builds the midrange 3X products, and the Entry System Division, which builds the PC, the PS/2, and the soon-to-be-inherited high-performance UNIX-based RT PC, would also enhance their programmers' productivity, if a consistent set of application enabling software were available.

Any improvement in programmer productivity would have a huge financial impact. STL, the Systems Product Division, and the Entry Systems Division together were spending roughly $2 billion annually on software R&D for the 370, 3X, and PC product lines. A single-digit improvement in productivity would be equivalent to the addition of millions of dollars to the R&D budget. A double-digit improvement would add even more.

While Taradalsky was sure that consistent application enabling common software across the three divisions' hardware environments was theoretically possible, he was not sure how it could be practically accomplished. After some reflection he made two important points.

First, to create consistent application enabling software across different kinds of computers, the application enabling software must be insulated from all the operating systems. IBM had never attempted this before and would have to find a way to accomplish that goal.

Wheeler agreed with half of what Taradalsky had said. Yes, the application enabling software would have to be buffered from the operating system. He then told Taradalsky he had a solution to that problem—a body of interfaces. This proposal piqued Taradalsky's interest.

Wheeler suggested that a body of interfaces could be created that would buffer the application enabling software from the operating systems. That body of interfaces could be called the common programming interface. Wheeler placed a transparency on the overhead projector. An image like the one in Figure 1 appeared on the wall.

Taradalsky agreed with the concept, theoretically. A buffer could be created between the operating systems and the application enabling software. He wondered who would be assigned to develop the buffer. Who would be selected to develop what Wheeler called the common programming interface (CPI).

Not waiting for an answer and not wanting to sound negative, Taradalsky told Wheeler that the greater the number of operating systems, the greater the complexity and magnitude of the task, and the greater the number of interfaces. Wheeler's proposed common programming interface might have to include a lot of interfaces—like those for MVS, VM, VSE, PC-DOS, AIX, OS/2, and others. That would be a tremendous job!

Wheeler agreed that including all the operating systems constituted too large a task. He advised Taradalsky to think about how the scope could be limited to just a few operating systems; namely, the operating environments of the 370 MVS, VM, the 3X follow-on product, and PS/2. Other operating systems could be added later. Developing interfaces for four operating systems was a big job, but at least it could be accomplished.

The operating systems that Wheeler suggested made good business sense. Because of enhancements made to

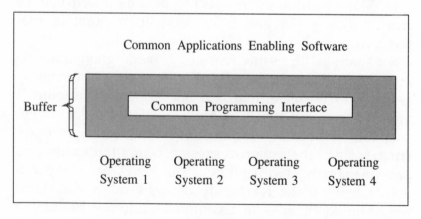

Figure 1 – Common Programming Interface Buffer

MVS and VM, these two products now outclass their previous peer product, VSE. The gap between these operating systems will continue to widen in the future. Because VSE is such an old operating system and because it has so few users—roughly 20,000—it would be difficult for IBM to make a business case for including it under SAA. Though IBM would like to migrate these customers, it can't. Including VME in the common programming interface unfortunately, would not push those users into the VM environment. On the other hand, the MVS and VM are money-making environments.

Including the 3X follow-on product rather than the S/36 and S/38 also made good business sense. Technically, the S/36 operating system was obsolete and could not meet emerging requirements for highly integrated, data-intensive networks that customers wanted to build. The S/38 operating system represented world-class technology but had a relatively small customer base. The 3X follow-on product to be announced in 1988 would allow S/36 and S/38 users to migrate to that product.

For many of the same reasons, it made good business sense not to include the IBM PC. The PC-DOS operating system was obsolete. It would not work well in today's, much less tomorrow's, highly integrated, data-intensive computer networks. Customers preferred an operating system that offered greater communications and data management capabilities. The UNIX-based operating system on the RT family of technical workstations was omitted because of its limited customer base. Selling high-performance workstations based on the OS/2 operating system would be more profitable. It therefore made sense to focus on the new OS/2 multifunction operating system.

Taradalsky thought of another point. If the CPI serves as a buffer between application enabling programs and the operating systems, it must also interact with communications software as well as the software that presents and requests information.

Wheeler agreed. The CPI would serve as the interface between the application enabling software and all major layers of software. Wheeler added that the CPI can be thought of as a buffer not just between application enabling software and the other major software layers, but between people and machines.

"People and machines?"

"Yes, the CPI will buffer the programmer from the operating system and the hardware. The programmer uses resources of the CPI that are common to all three hardware environments. It won't matter to the programmer whether an OS/2 and VM environment, an OS/2 and 3X follow-on product's operating system, or an OS/2, 3X, VM and MVS environment are below the buffer. All the tools he needs will be part of the CPI."

Taradalsky knew then that the CPI held the key to a major advance in computing.

Sensing Taradalsky's approval, Wheeler added that the hardware, operating system, communications software, and user access were all subject to change. However, the CPI would preclude changes that affect the application enabling software. As a result, the programmer, the application software, and the user will remain unaffected.

By this time, Taradalsky was convinced that Wheeler and IBM were serious about driving software consistency across the three hardware environments. He had to wonder about the next step.

The Task Forces

Wheeler announced that Common User Access Interface, Common Communications Support, Common Programming Interface, and Common Applications Task Forces would evaluate the feasibility of the project. They would be headed by high–level development executives from the Entry Systems Division, Communication Products Division, the General Products Division, and the Software Development Group of IIS, respectively. All task force leaders would continue to report to the management of their division, but they would also report to Wheeler. The structure of the organization appears in Figure 2.

Taradalsky would head the Common Programming Interface Task Force. Wheeler wanted Taradalsky's for this slot for several reasons. Taradalsky had the resources of STL at his command, and he had experience in developing very complex systems. In addition, Taradalsky was known as *Mr. Performance*. Wheeler fully expected performance problems to occur, as they do with any new system, and Morris knew that Taradalsky could solve them. Wheeler wanted him on the project from its inception.

When Wheeler offered Taradalsky the chance to form the Common Programming Interface Task Force, he accepted immediately. The task force would give him an opportunity to study and possibly attack the

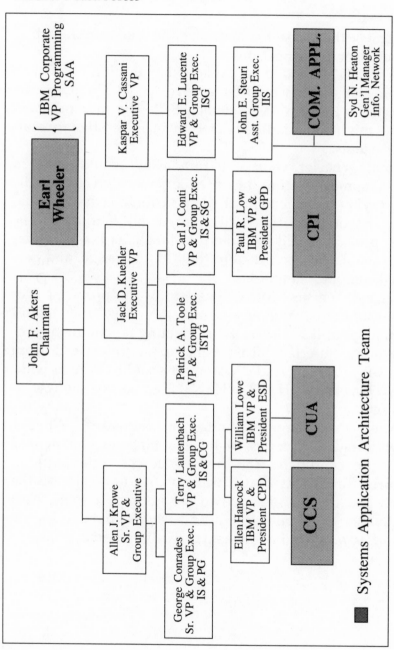

Figure 2 – IBM's Systems Application Architecture Team

biggest technical problem facing the IBM programming
community.

Wheeler proceeded to explain that the initial mission
of the task forces would be to develop the CPI across the
370, the follow-on 3X, and the PS/2. The mission statement might be modified later to include other operating systems.

First, Wheeler went on, Taradalsky would have to
select someone from his own organization to handle
day-to-day management of the task force activities. That
person would be the focal point of all staffing efforts.
The project would be interdivisional, and representatives would be needed from the 370, midrange, and personal computer families.

Second, the task forces must study the problem, propose solutions, and advise Wheeler how they would
then accomplish the task of creating a common programming interface. This initial plan to expand from
the 370 to the PC and 3X families should be done within six weeks. "WHAT? WHEN?" Taradalsky thought to
himself.

After a few more minutes of discussion, Wheeler
gave Taradalsky copies of the planning documents and
a list of candidates for the task forces. Wheeler then
assured Taradalsky that it was good to have him on the
team and that he expected to see his report soon. With
that, the two men stood and shook hands. Morris
Taradalsky hurried to catch an early flight home.

13 The Way To San Jose

THE FRIENDLY SKIES—EARLY 1987

Morris Taradalsky returned to California with the deeper implications of Wheeler's proposal surfacing in his mind. He was not comfortable with all that he thought.

Morris sensed the magnitude of the impact of Wheeler's strategy. It could have the same impact that the deregulation of the telephone industry had on AT&T. AT&T employees had had to learn how to think in a competitive environment rather than a regulated one. IBM employees would not have to learn how to think competitively, but they would have to learn how to think differently.

If the company went ahead, and Taradalsky now strongly suspected that it would attempt to implement common software across the three hardware families, a lot of people in IBM would be required to change their way of thinking. Not everyone would be able to do that. And he might be the first in line to have to make that change. That in itself made Taradalsky feel uncomfortable.

Before pursuing these thoughts, Taradalsky asked himself a crucial question. "Did Earl Wheeler, himself, have the force to make this happen?"

"No," thought Taradalsky. "No one person, especially someone who is not head of the corporation, someone who is not captain of the ship, could grab the wheel of a ship this big and attempt a near U-turn. Even the captain would need, at a minimum, the full support of the first mate and the rest of the bridge. But if Wheeler had the full support of the ship's captain and first lieutenants, he might have a chance to do it." Did he have that support?

Obviously, Wheeler did have commitment from the top. He would not have asked Taradalsky to form an interdivisional task force without the support of Taradalsky's boss and the presidents of the other divisions, whose people Wheeler had suggested should be on the task force. Wheeler wouldn't call up task forces, get dozens—maybe even hundreds—of people flying on airplanes, meeting for hours, studying data, writing reports, and giving presentations unless, at the least, the three most powerful men in the company were prepared to help Wheeler change direction when the time came.

He must have the support of the Management Committee. If not the entire MC, he must have the support of the three key members—Akers, Kuehler, and Krowe. These were the top three men of the company at that time. And didn't Wheeler say that the company, not he, himself, had decided to mobilize the task forces?

Yes, he had. As soon as Taradalsky recalled this, he dismissed the thought that Wheeler might be working on his own.

Differing Perspectives

Taradalsky knew that most IBM developers practiced what could be called a vertical way of thinking, perhaps because they had grown so accustomed to thinking up and down a product line (see Figure 1). IBMers and, for that matter, most people usually list a family of products from the smallest model to the largest in a vertical format. Then they make millions of decisions about the products on the lists. Since the list is presented vertically and since they make so many decisions with respect to that list, it is not unusual that they think vertically.

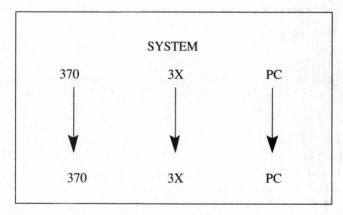

Figure 1 – Vertical Product Orientation

Vertical thinking is reinforced by IBM's drive to make those product lines a success. Huge walls in the organizational structure separate each division. The demands are so great within a division that no one has time to venture beyond the wall. Even IBM developers who transfer to different divisions, which happens frequently, still continue to think vertically. All that changes is the products on the list.

Taradalsky was no exception. For his entire IBM career, he had focused strictly on programming requirements for the high-end 370 families of products. Taradalsky had prowled up and down the 370 product line. He had never ventured over the boundary to the other two product lines. General Product Division's constant marching orders had left him little time to daydream about the needs of the 3X and personal computer families. This twenty-year, single-product focus had nailed down a well-developed, vertical way of thinking.

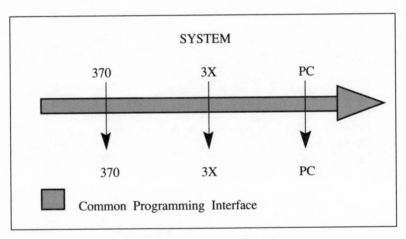

Figure 2 – CPI Across the Three Hardware Environments

Taradalsky realized he would have to reorient his thinking—from vertical to horizontal. At the very least he would have to incorporate some horizontal thinking into his repertoire. While it is said that you can't teach an old dog new tricks, Taradalsky was an experienced IBM development executive. Give him some time to study a problem and he'd give it a good try.

If Wheeler's proposal went through, Taradalsky would have to line up the three products in his mind and think horizontally across product lines (see Figure 2). He would have to scale the wall mentally between the 370 and the 3X, and the 370 and personal computer to think about problems that could develop for each group. He would have to think actively about the application enabling needs of each division's mainline products. The rest of Santa Teresa Labs would have to make this difficult shift as well.

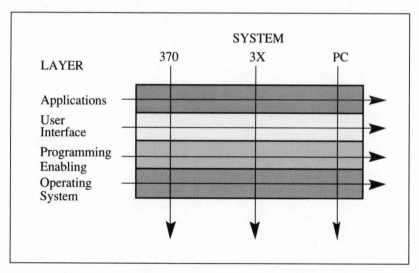

Figure 3 – IBM's New Thinking Across Three Hardware Environments

Flying home, Taradalsky expanded his thinking beyond the developers working on application enabling products to include all other programmers throughout the company. Applications programmers working on applications would have to think about the ramifications of their work on all three product lines. Programmers working on user access interfaces would have to think about the application of their work across all hardware environments. The same would be true for programmers supporting operating systems. If Wheeler's plan flew, the perspective illustrated in Figure 3 would soon become pervasive throughout the IBM organization.

14 Back Home Again

SETTING UP THE CPI TASK FORCE

Back home in San Jose, Taradalsky realized that Wheeler had not given him much time to get comfortable with all the demands—six weeks! In six weeks, he wanted the Common Programming Interface Task Force created, staffed, and ready to meet with him in Purchase, New York. That wasn't much time at all.

Wheeler told Taradalsky that whoever headed the team would have to get on a plane at least once a month. That person would have to know a lot about data bases, especially relational data bases like DB2. This sounded like a job for one of Taradalsky's best men!

Taradalsky's best man turned out to be a woman—Carol Schira. He selected her for her strong background in relational data bases and her firsthand experience with interfaces. She had been the product manager for the user interface to the DB2 data base,

QMF. Taradalsky knew Wheeler would like her—he is soft spoken, polite, gentle, understated, but strong; Carol had the same qualities.

Task Force Meeting

Six weeks later, Taradalsky returned to Purchase accompanied by Carol Schira and some other members of the newly created Common Programming Interface Task Force.

Taradalsky and Schira told Wheeler how they planned to attack the problem of creating a common programming interface. Schira explained that they had asked themselves the obvious—what common resources do programmers need across the three hardware environments? Once they asked that question, the answers just fell out. Programmers need languages to write programs and some services to facilitate the process. Programmers would want a common set of languages supported across the three environments. They would want a set of common services, such as utility programs, that they could use when needed. They told Wheeler that the task force should concentrate on determining which languages and services would be needed across each of the three hardware environments— languages and services were the key to the development of the common programming interface.

Schira discussed the different types of languages that programmers use. These include application generators (languages especially suited for the development of applications); traditional high-level languages (such as

COBOL); and procedural languages (languages particularly suited for command procedures, user-defined macros such as the Dialog Manager, editor subcommands, prototyping, and personal computing). If the programmer interfaces were provided for these types of languages, all the language needs of the programmers would be accommodated.

Wheeler agreed with these subcategories for languages and then asked whether the team had worked out the subcategories to be included under services.

Schira replied that four services (computer utilities) had been identified as timesaving aids for programmers: dialog services, presentation services, query services, and software interfaces. Dialog services help programmers to display and control user interaction with panels that contain constant and variable information on a screen. They include menu selections, help information, data requests and messages, and the passing of data and function requests from the user to the application. Query services allow a user to access information in a data base and to control how the data are displayed. Presentation services enable a programmer to call up other functions of the Presentation Manager. The SQL (relational data base) interface at the front end of the Data Manager is a typical software interface. Through its use, programmers can eliminate the writing of line after line of code to define and then access the data base.

Wheeler approved the team's general approach, but he asked the Common Programming Interface Task Force to inventory all the existing programs and services offered by each of the product lines to see if any other languages and services might have to be included in the common programming interface. Wheeler also suggested that they talk to Peter Dance; he could help them determine which languages and services customers would want from any or all of the three families.

The task force was scheduled to meet again within six weeks or sooner. And they did. They met roughly every six weeks for the remainder of the year—right up to Wheeler's February 18 presentation meeting.

15 Taradalsky on Second

Several weeks before the February 18 meeting, the Common Programming Interface Task Force approached the software product managers for commitments on the languages and services to be included in the initial announcement. Taradalsky reported on the status of that effort at the meeting.

On the overhead projector, Taradalsky placed a transparency (Figure 1) that listed the languages to be supported under SAA. The first item showed three high-level languages: COBOL, FORTRAN, and C. He then reported that the product managers had agreed to support these languages across the three product lines. Someone clapped.

Peter Dance was pleased and he said so. Many of the Fortune 100 companies use all three hardware environments. They have invested multiple millions of dollars in COBOL-based data processing and FORTRAN-based

engineering/scientific applications. Some were building applications based on C. Marketing could now announce that IBM will offer consistent tools, especially
to large customers, that would reduce programming
costs and minimize the applications backlog. Including
these three languages in the initial SAA announcement would alert large companies to the importance of
SAA and its potential.

Dance was also pleased that Taradalsky received commitments to support those languages across the three
SAA hardware environments. He knew that many software companies have expertise in one or more of those
languages but that they usually restricted their work to
one type of hardware—370–size equipment, midrange
machines, or personal computers. Announcing support
of these three popular languages across the IBM hardware environments would enable software developers
to leverage *their* expertise as well!

LANGUAGES
- Common higher-level languages supported
  - COBOL based on ANS Programming Language,
    COBOL X3.23—1985
  - FORTRAN based on ANS Programming
    Language FORTRAN 77 Level
  - C based on the draft proposed by ANS
    Standard (X3J11)
- Application generator based on an element of
  Cross Systems Product (CSP)
- Procedures language based on the existing REXX
  language

Figure 1 – SAA-Supported Languages

Saranga had a question—Who would put COBOL on the PS/2? Everyone wanted COBOL on the PS/2, but no one offered to do it. Hanrahan had responsibility for PS/2 software, but his programmers had no real experience in developing languages. Also, he was busy managing the development of the Presentation Manager, the Data Manager, and the extended version of OS/2 operating system. Taradalsky was responsible for the SAA common programming interface across all three hardware families and for 370 languages; however, that did not mean that he had to implement the language for that interface. Also, while Santa Teresa supported COBOL on the 370, that was no reason to expect it to implement COBOL on any other family of machines. Besides, Taradalsky's staff's resources were already severely constrained. Saranga, Taradalsky's old boss from the Poughkeepsie days, wanted to know how this issue had been resolved and who would head the project.

Taradalsky answered Saranga, stating that he would be responsible for implementing COBOL on the PS/2.

Saranga questioned who in Santa Teresa would head the project. He knew that Taradalsky couldn't personally manage the completion of COBOL/PS/2.

Taradalsky briefly explained that the best solution, in his judgment, was to retain a software company that specialized in COBOL compilers to do the job. Saranga, Wheeler, and the others concurred.

The RPG (report program generator) language for System/36 users was another area of contention. John Friedline—Mr. System/36 of IBM—having rolled out the system to the marketplace on May 16, 1983, asked whether Taradalsky had a commitment to support RPG. The System/36 is the most successful midrange computer the world has ever seen, and RPG is by far the most popular language for it. It is possible that Friedline's contribution to the success of the System/36 qualified him to manage the roll out of the SAA to the field.

Taradalsky shook his head no and was ready to move on to the next item, but a lively discussion erupted. Friedline reminded everyone that the System/36 customer base is huge—more than 250,000 systems; that those customers had invested millions, perhaps billions, in RPG-based applications software; and that announcing COBOL, FORTRAN, and C under SAA would help only a small percentage of those customers —those who had written applications with those languages. How would the other customers be supported?

Someone asked about the composition of the System /36 customer base. Either Friedline or Dance replied that a great percentage of the System/36 users are single establishments that don't usually have a second computer other than PCs. The rest are very large customers, those with several 370s, that use some System/36s as departmental processors or in satellite facilities.

Dance interrupted the debate by asking which customer would have the greatest immediate need for SAA. After a few silent moments, one participant responded that the largest companies, especially those with more than one family of IBM computers, would have the greatest immediate need for SAA. No one disagreed with that statement. Someone added that just about everyone in that group has at least one 370 and in the very near future almost all of them will have PS/2s as well. The implication was that not everyone who had two systems would have an RPG system.

Then Wheeler asked why the RPG product manager would not commit to support RPG under SAA. Taradalsky explained that while IBM will eventually support RPG in all SAA environments, right now no one has determined the best technical solution to the problem. When the product manager is sure that there is a good plan and that it can be implemented within two years from announcement, he will commit to SAA.

Wheeler then said the midrange is key. However, if the RPG people need more time to work out the technical problems, give them the time. Reluctantly, RPG would be omitted from the initial announcement.

Taradalsky also informed the meeting that PL/1 would not be included as part of SAA. Few IBM customers in the United States use PL/1. Worldwide, Europeans use it more than North Americans do. If marketing studies indicted that PL/1 should be included in SAA, his staff would evaluate the need.

Next in his presentation, Taradalsky reported that the initial SAA announcement would not specify the AI languages that IBM would support across the three families. Wheeler didn't like that; nor did Dance.

Dance repeated what Taradalsky had heard a dozen times before: Many of the software companies developing AI tools or applications were demanding AI support from IBM. If IBM could not provide the tools, it should at least state the direction of its AI support. Large users were expressing the same demands. An SAA commitment to AI would give the market what it needed. Others agreed that IBM needed to reveal which AI languages it would support across the three families. LISP? PROLOG? Others?

Taradalsky then explained that the selection of AI

tools is more complex than meets the eye. AI tools must work with data bases. When data base issues are considered, a complex problem arises. His staff has been trying to understand the requirements for AI support across the three environments, but had reached no conclusions.

"But do you have any good news about AI tools?" he was asked.

Taradalsky responded that, besides several internal IBM developments, it was likely that IBM could offer other software companies' AI tools under IBM's logo. His staff had been working with a number of software companies, among them, Intellicorp of Mountain View, California. In time, IBM would announce AI software across the three families, but it could not announce any specific products now.

Earl Wheeler supported Taradalsky's position. The development side of the business could make no specific statements at this time. However, since IBM was committed to supporting AI tools under SAA, that should be specifically stated in the announcement. All agreed. They agreed that the initial announcement of SAA would include a reference that IBM was committed to adding AI software development tools to the SAA offering.

Returning to the overhead projector, Taradalsky pointed to the second item on the slide and stated that one application generator language would be offered as part of SAA. It would be based on elements of the Cross Systems Product (CSP) application generator language.

Wheeler said he was extremely delighted that Taradalsky had been able to get the product manager of the CSP application development language to agree to support her product across the three environments. One of the main goals of SAA was to provide customers with the tools needed to make it easy for them to generate applications across multiple product lines. It would look shabby to announce SAA without a highly efficient language that enabled users to write in one environment and execute in another.

Taradalsky had glanced over at Mike Saranga when Wheeler made his comment. Taradalsky just looked, but a smile slowly grew on Saranga's face.

The application generator belonged to Saranga. For some time, Saranga had put off making this commitment. Taradalsky and Carol Schira, even Earl Wheeler himself, had had a difficult time getting Saranga to guarantee that his organization would support the language across the three hardware environments and do so in a timely manner. Saranga kept asking for more time to study the problem before he and Martha Rivers, his product manager, signed on. He had a lot of justification for holding off.

The application generator based on CSP eventually had to run on the 3X follow-on product's operating system and on the OS/2. Martha Rivers couldn't get her hands on enough stable 3X follow-on and OS/2 technology to be sure she understood the problem. She lacked several pieces of the technology she needed before she could design, much less think about testing, an application generator in the 3X and OS/2 environments. At some point, she and Saranga capitulated. Now Saranga had two years to produce.

Morris Taradalsky suggested that any questions about the application generator to be based on CSP should be directed to Mike Saranga when he made his presentation. Taradalsky expected Saranga to cut in anyway, if anyone had any questions about CSP. It's sometimes good to offer the stage before it's taken away from you.

Pointing to the last item on the transparency, Taradalsky calmly said he had a commitment for a procedures language. The REXX product manager had agreed to support REXX across the three environments. Taradalsky smiled when he said that. Probably only those who work with procedural languages appreciate the importance of including them in the initial SAA announcement and appreciate Taradalsky's smile. They are not a common item.

At this point, Taradalsky summarized: IBM was offering three higher-level languages, one application generator, and a procedures language—a hefty offering, in his opinion. Not everyone agreed.

Taradalsky replaced the slide with another that looked like Figure 2, saying that he would now review the common services that would be offered with the initial SAA announcement. What he said next triggered a response from everyone.

"I have a commitment from the three relational data base managers that they will all use the same interface on the front end of their data bases. That will, of course, be the international standard—SQL."

Wheeler asked the first question, looking at both Taradalsky, who had the responsibility of selecting the services that would be offered with CPI, and Hanrahan, who had responsibility for developing the Data Manager. Wheeler wanted to make doubly sure there was no problem developing the Data Manager with an SQL programmer's interface. It was another major piece of technology that IBM needed to enable customers to build applications efficiently on the PS/2. And that technology was a critical element in the plan to build the large base of IBM users that would create the cooperative processing environment.

Wheeler asked if everything was going okay in developing the Data Manager with SQL

Hanrahan reviewed the progress of the Data Manager, explaining what had been accomplished and what was left undone. He thanked Taradalsky for the loan of the DB2 relational data base programmers who had helped his Austin programmers with the design and implementation of the relational model. Hanrahan now understood and appreciated why Wheeler had pushed so hard for a data base management system that utilizes a relational model on OS/2. He said that in the near future, customers are going to build PC-based applications that require gigabits of DASD. The old se-

---

SERVICES

◆ Data Base Interface will be based on the ANS
  Data Base Language, Structured Query Language
  (SQL) X3.135—1986, and IBM's SQL

◆ Query Interface will be based on an "extension
  of the interfaces" in the existing Query
  Management Facility (QMF) Product

◆ Presentation Interface will be based on "extensions
  to the interface in key elements" of today's
  Graphical Data Display Manager (GDDM)product

◆ Dialog Interface will be based on "extensions to
  the interface" in today's EZ–VU

Figure 2 – SAA-Supported Services

quential file approaches would be too awkward to use. That was the essence of the argument that Wheeler had used to persuade others in ESD that a relational data base for the OS/2 was the way to go.

Wheeler then asked Taradalsky for the big picture—What it does mean, now that all the IBM relational data base product managers have agreed to provide the SQL programmers interface?

Taradalsky summed up the progress so far. "The product managers of all three of the company's data base management systems have agreed to support SQL. The relational data base management system DB2, of course, supports SQL. The data base management system offered with the 3X follow-on and the extended version of the OS/2 (the Data Manager) will offer the SQL interface. That means that the same interface will be available on each of the three operating environments." Still showing no excitement, but referencing the diagram in Figure 3, he said that programmers could easily write programs that could interconnect heterogeneous data bases, making it possible to build cooperative processing systems and to interconnect applications.

Although Taradalsky showed no excitement over that last point, Wheeler exclaimed enthusiastically that what Morris had just said was significant! For the visitors in the back of room, Wheeler added that if all DBMSs had the same programming interface, a *common* interface, programmers would not have to learn different commands whenever they switched from one DBMS-related project to another. When programmers addressed the Data Manager, they would see only SQL. When they addressed the 3X follow-on products' data base management system, they would see the same interface. This would remove a major obstacle facing anyone who wanted to build cooperative processing or enterprisewide systems.

Before Wheeler returned the floor to Taradalsky, he looked at Hanrahan and said: "Are you sure that we'll have the Data Manager/SQL by the end of 1988?"

Hanrahan replied: "Don't worry. You'll have it."

Just as Taradalsky was about to continue, someone in the back of the room asked a question. "How will SQL work with the IMS data base?" Even the Tommy Newsome look-alike smiled a little at this question.

Taradalsky respectfully replied that by definition and design, SQL relates strictly to relational data bases. IMS is not a relational data base; therefore, it will not work with SQL.

Mike Saranga then spoke out. "The real issue here is the lack of a common programming interface for IMS. It's great that programmers will have a common inter-

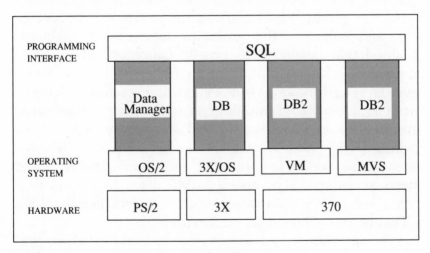

Figure 3 – Common Programming Interface

face for all three relational data bases—that will save millions of hours—but it won't help the guy that also runs IMS."

Saranga continued. He pointed to Taradalsky's list of SAA services projected on the wall. "What are you going to do? There's no common programming interface for IMS."

"That's correct," said Taradalsky. "CPI isn't available for IMS, and that's why we are not offering it as part of SAA at this time." He explained that to offer a common programming interface for IMS would require getting the product manager for the PS/2 DBMS and the product manager for the 3X follow-on products' DBMS to first agree to SQL and then to implement the IMS interface. That would be too much to expect them to take on at this time. Morris continued, "Even if they agreed to support the IMS interface, the common communications support is not in place. Without the communications support, no one could access those interfaces."

At this point, Wheeler spoke up, saying: "We can't go out and solve all the problems immediately." He explained that he, too, was greatly concerned about making it easy for programmers to utilize IMS in a multi-system environment, but everything couldn't happen at once. He asked Taradalsky to review what other steps had been taken to accommodate IMS programmers.

Taradalsky had to search for a moment. Then he mentioned that a few months ago, some products had been announced that enabled IMS users to extract data from their IMS data bases and build relational tables. "That helps IMS users to work with DB2."

Wheeler then asked Don Casey to state what he was doing to make it easier for programmers to use IMS in a multisystem environment. Casey, who had been thinking of something else when this discussion was going on, asked Wheeler to repeat the question. After Wheeler restated the question, Casey responded that he was working on it. His division was studying the communications support needed to enable programmers in a multisystem environment to address IMS data bases. His staff was trying to determine how to make LU6.2 program-to-program communication support interact with IMS. As Casey explained: When a program evokes LU6.2, LU6.2 looks for the other program and says: "Here, take control." However, IMS is a program that first puts all requests into a queue. It could be a while before IMS is ready to accept the LU6.2 call." Casey continued that his LU6.2 product was not designed to wait in a queue. This causes a lot of system problems.

Wheeler then asked Casey: "When can we expect a solution to this problem? When can we expect to make it easier for programmers in a multisystem environment to be able to call up IMS?"

Casey answered: "No promises, but maybe marketing will be able to announce some communications support for IMS under the SAA framework around June 1987."

At this point Saranga said: "I sure hope so. A lot of IMS users are going to think we have abandoned them if we don't announce something for IMS under SAA."

Dance agreed that as soon after the initial SAA announcement as possible, they would have to start pulling IMS under the SAA umbrella.

The discussion continued for several minutes. Everyone understood the problem better. Part of the time the discussion was going on, Taradalsky sat down to rest his feet. As soon as he saw the opportunity, he stood and said there really was only one more thing he wanted to say.

Taradalsky then briefly commented on the Query Management Facility (QMF), Presentation Interface, and Dialog Interface. Product managers had committed to support these interfaces across the three families. This should help programmers write programs that issue queries and present text and graphical data on the displays.

When Taradalsky asked for questions again, no one responded. Deferring to Wheeler, who thanked him for doing a good job. Taradalsky took his seat. Earl Wheeler added that IBM had taken a big step toward implementing common programming languages across three disparate hardware environments—a step toward a common programming interface.

To himself he said "Two down, two to go."

16 Casey at Bat

The focus of the group shifted to Don Casey. Casey smiled, stood, and walked around the table to the overhead projector. He looked pale, but he was relaxed.

Why wouldn't Casey be at ease? He had been in this room many times, he had known Taradalsky and Saranga since the MVS days in Poughkeepsie, and he and Dick Hanrahan were old buddies who'd visited each other's homes a dozen times. He also knew that Wheeler never springs unfair surprises on people and understands the challenges of developing communication software. But there were two other reasons for Casey's relaxed demeanor this morning.

First, Casey's work at the Communications Product Division had forced him to develop an across-the-product-line perspective long ago. CPD, through the seventies, had concentrated on providing communications support to interconnect the various members of the 370 families. In the early eighties, CPD broadened its focus

159

to include the PC family and the existing 3X family. By providing connectivity across the three hardware lines, CPD had a natural cross-systems product focus that the other divisions lacked. So Casey was more comfortable with Wheeler's horizontal way of thinking than any of the other development VPs in the room.

Second, Casey had more time to prepare for this morning's meeting. In early 1986, IBM felt the pressure from customers as well as the rest of the industry. The market believed increasingly that IBM was offering closed systems and that competitors were offering open systems.

Digital Equipment Corporation (DEC), in particular exacerbated this situation. DEC, sooner and certainly more loudly and more firmly than any other supplier announced its support of Open Systems Interconnect (OSI), the international standard for interconnection of computer systems. IBM took its time announcing its support for the creation of standards and included an important qualifier: basically, IBM would support those OSI standards that made business sense to IBM. The late announcement and the qualifier helped convince people that IBM did not really support OSI or openness.

The pressure became unbearable when a few loud and powerful multinationals, some European companies and government agencies, and a few U.S. government agencies announced their intention to purchase only computer systems that were open. Not all of those enterprises considered IBM's SNA open enough for them. So, they increasingly built OSI requirements into their bids. This situation convinced IBM that it had to assure customers and the industry that IBM was open, too.

IBM Begins to Open Up

The Management Committee, through Terry Lautenbach, who was Group Vice President of Entry Systems Division and the Communications Product Division, asked Ellen Hancock to review CPD's offerings for 370, 3X, and PC divisions in terms of the requirements for open systems. Hancock immediately called Don Casey, Don Heile, Bill Warner, and several other CPD executives to help her assess the status of IBM's openness. Shortly after submitting their report, they plugged a few holes, and, in September 1986, IBM announced to the public that its systems were "open, have been open, and will continue to be open." IBM backed its statement by listing numerous parts of its architecture to which other suppliers could interconnect.

The September 1986 open systems statement of direction fulfilled 90% or more of Wheeler's requirements for SAA common communications support. Casey did not have to struggle to prepare for the February meeting—he could have spent the last week or so getting some sun on Fort Lauderdale beaches. All he had to do was to make a few changes to previously designed slides and he was ready for his presentation to Wheeler.

Casey Signs On

Like Taradalsky, Casey had been invited to a one-on-one with Wheeler long before the term Systems Application Architecture was coined. But unlike Taradalsky,

Casey had known what to expect; Ellen Hancock had briefed him. So what Wheeler told him was not a surprise.

At the meeting, Wheeler switched on an overhead projector that sat on the right side of his desk. Casey sat next to him and the projector, while Wheeler flashed a dozen transparencies onto the light blue office walls. When they finished viewing the slides, he asked Casey to develop the common communications support that would enable application programmers, systems programmers, and systems analysts to effectively interconnect the applications programs, systems, and devices across IBM's three product lines. Casey, recognizing the importance of what Wheeler had shown him, agreed to adjust the direction of the programmers under him to support Wheeler's plan.

Updating the Seven-Layer Model

At that and subsequent meetings, Casey and Wheeler decided that some of the seven-layer SNA model could be used to categorize the type of communications support that SAA would offer. They needed data streams, applications services, session services, network, and data link control categories. Also, Wheeler told him that SNA was and still is a wonderful architecture. However, without the management system, it would never have become so important. Wheeler wanted Casey to become a member of the Systems Application Architecture management team.

Casey accepted. Wheeler gave him the assignment to form a task force and to restudy the common communications support needed to support the interconnection of systems and applications across the PS/2, 3X follow-on, and 370 families.

Casey Reports

At the February 18, 1987 meeting, Casey was expected to explain the communications support his division would provide for the three hardware environments and the four operating systems environments. He first showed a transparency titled *Common Communications Support–SAA* and began to introduce his division's support:

"Ellen Hancock and CPD's product managers have signed up to support common communications support (CCS), which will consist of extensions to existing communications architectures. It will be based on SNA and 'selected' international standards, will support distributed functions, and will be consistent with open communications architecture. The architectures selected have been chosen largely from SNA and international standards, and each was included in IBM's open communications architectures announcement of September 16, 1986. While additional communications architectures will be considered for inclusion in CCS in the future, I will now identify the currently announced support."

At this point, Casey placed a second transparency (Figure 1) on the glass face of the overhead projector. He leaned against the desk and pointed to *Data Streams*, which was reflected on the pale yellow wall. The initial common communications support of SAA would include three different data streams across the three hardware environments.

Data Streams

Inclusion of the 3270 data stream was no surprise to anyone. How would the millions of 3270 terminals in the 370 environment become part of SAA without the support of the 3270 data stream? Anything as all-encompassing as SAA has to accommodate the most popular 370-based terminal. Someone asked which data stream would accommodate the most popular 3X terminal and workstation—the 5250. Heated discussion ensued.

"The System/36 users are going to think we don't care about them if we don't indicate data stream support for the 5250..."

"We can't commit to it now..."

"We have to add 5250 data stream support to the 3X follow-on product."

It was finally decided that no mention of the 5250 would be made in the initial SAA announcement, although that decision was reversed only a few weeks later.

DCA was also no surprise to anyone in the room. The addition of DCA meant that programmers across the three product lines could use the same rules for specifying the form and meaning of a textual document, which would provide a uniform interchange of textual information in the office environment and make it easier to revise documents without rekeying data.

Intelligent printer data stream is a high-function data stream intended for use with all-points-addressable, very high-speed page printers. Including it in the initial SAA announcement meant that all three hardware environments could address various printers in a system. No one commented about this common communications support feature.

Application Services

Casey rambled on about the application services that would be part of the initial SAA announcement: SNA Distributed Services (SNADS), Document Interchange Architecture (DIA), and SNA Network Management Architecture.

SNADS, which controls the distribution of information among systems in a multisystem network, would provide an asynchronous distribution capability, thereby avoiding the need for active sessions between the end points. The inclusion of SNADS in SAA meant that IBM would continue to extend this service across the three hardware environments.

DIA defines the rules for document distribution and library services: for filing, retrieving, searching, and distributing all kinds of information. The addition of DIA in SAA simply meant that all IBM office products participating in SAA would utilize this architecture.

SNA Network Management Architecture describes IBM's approach to managing communication networks. The protocols of problem management offer a vehicle for monitoring network operations from a cen-

- ◆ Data Streams
  3270 Data Stream
  Document Content Architecture (DCA)
  Intelligent Printer Data Stream (IPDS)
- ◆ Application Services
  SNA Distributed Services (SNADS)
  Document Interchange Architecture (DIA)
  SNA Network Management Architecture
- ◆ Session Services
  LU Type 6.2
- ◆ Network
  Low–Entry Networking Node (LEN)
- ◆ Data Link Controls
  Synchronous Data Link Control (SDLC)
  IBM Token–Ring Network
  X.25

Figure 1 – Common Communications Support

tral location. As customers' networks have grown in complexity and importance, so has the need to manage the networks, i.e., to determine what's happening in the network, how much this or that costs, what's broken or breaking. The statement that SNA Network Management would be supported under SAA simply assured customers that IBM would continue to develop its network management offering across the three hardware environments.

Session Services

Casey then commented on the session services that would be offered. CCS, he said, would support LU6.2 technology—which surprised no one. Since 1982, IBM had been supporting LU6.2 for program-to-program communications. LU6.2 defines a rich set of interprogram communication services, including base and optional supplementary services. Support of the base is included in all IBM LU6.2 products that expose an LU6.2 application programming interface. This facilitates compatibility of communications functions across systems.

"Will LU6.2 work with IMS?"

"No."

"Why not?"

"IMS communications is based on queueing. When LU6.2 calls a program, it expects immediate response. It doesn't expect to be placed in a queue."

"We are trying to find a way to make LU6.2 work with IMS. Possibly later this year we'll have something."

Network

Casey briefly stated that CCS for peer-to-peer communications would be provided by low–entry networking nodes (Type 2.1). Type 2.1 nodes can be either programmable or fixed-function systems. SNA low–entry networking allows, through a common set of protocols, multiple and parallel SNA sessions to be established between Type 2.1 nodes that are directly attached to each other.

Data Link Controls

When Casey pointed to Data Link Controls, he told the attendees that CCS would include Synchronous Data Link Control (SDLC), the Token-Ring Network, and X.25. SDLC is a discipline for managing synchronous, code-transparent, serial-by-bit information transfer between nodes that are joined by telecommunication links. IBM's Token-Ring Network consists of a wiring system, a set of communication adapters (stations), and an access protocol that controls the sharing of the physical medium by the stations attached to the LAN. X.25 defines a packet-mode interface for attaching data terminal equipment (DTE) such as host computers, communication controllers, and terminals to packet-switched data networks. Those in the room who knew what he was talking about said, "Of course." Those who did not, said the same.

More discussion!

"Does common communications support provide the basic underlying communications facility to interconnect the 370, 3X and PC families?"

"That's right."

"Sure the 3X is adequately supported?"

"Yes."

"We meet in six weeks to discuss how to support IMS better?"

"Sure."

"Don't forget to mention in the SAA announcement that we support OSI standards. Sales literature should emphasize that common communications support is an extension of what we have already developed in SNA, that we will keep enhancing SNA, and that we will incorporate OSI standards as they become available."

"Sure."

Casey placed another transparency on the overhead projector. It looked very much like Figure 2. The rectangle labeled Common Communications Support was in yellow. A previous transparency had also been bordered in yellow. Either Casey had a fondness for this color, or it had some other specific meaning to this group.

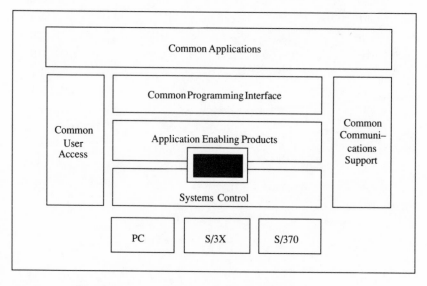

Figure 2 – IBM Systems Application Architecture

The transparency displayed a pictorial presentation of Systems Application Architecture. Casey pointed to the Common Communications Support block and demonstrated how SAA's common communications support addressed the needs of the common user access, application enabling products, and the common programming interface across the PC, 3X, and 370 families. With that, he turned off the projector, letting everyone know he was finished.

Wheeler thanked Casey as he returned to his seat. Wheeler knew he had the common programming interface and common communications support aspects of SAA nailed down for this afternoon's MC meeting.

Wheeler looked over at Mike Saranga. It was time for Saranga to make his contribution to the meeting.

17 Key Connection

SARANGA'S THREE ASSIGNMENTS
—EARLY 1986

About a year before, Wheeler had given Mike Saranga three assignments. Although Dick Hanrahan, Morris Taradalsky, and Don Casey had formed the foundation for an environment where application development productivity could be greatly enhanced, Wheeler wanted to focus management specifically on applications. To Wheeler, applications were the decisive point. It would be terrible if Hanrahan's work in developing a common user access, Taradalsky's work in developing the common programming interface, and Casey's work in developing common communications support somehow missed the mark. Without a breakthrough in application development, customers would continue to squander a fortune trying to implement software on previously acquired equipment. Companies that had cooperative processing as a distant objective would not be able to design their next-generation information systems based on IBM products, and IBM sales would continue to lag.

Common Applications Interface

The first of Saranga's three important assignments was to determine what technological developments were needed to create an environment where application programs could proliferate across the three hardware environments. Saranga needed to define the technical requirements for application development to (1) enable all IBM customers' application programmers to slash their company's applications backlog, (2) greatly expand the opportunity for software companies to develop applications for IBM hardware, and (3) improve the productivity of IBM's own application development effort. Clearly an easy, straightforward, closed-ended task— the kind of assignment where all Saranga had to do was to order another vanity license plate, place it on his car, and park the car where his staff could see it!

The definition of the common applications interface was Saranga's first priority. This definition would specify what Hanrahan's common user access, Taradalsky's common programming interface, and Casey's common communications support effort must provide. If Saranga could define the common applications interface, Wheeler and the four development executives could determine what would be technically feasible and practical, and the all of them would have a clear view of the target. He would be able to say to Dick Hanrahan: "This is what we need in a common user interface to make it attractive for software companies supporting Apple or DEC hardware to write PS/2 applications." He would be able to say to Morris Taradalsky: "The customers, software developers, and IBM developers need this mix of languages and programming services to slash through the applications backlog." And to Don Casey he could say: "For programmers to build applications that are really connected or that run on cooperative processing systems, here is the list of enhancements to SNA or additional OSI standards that you need to support."

Saranga and his staff studied the programming and services needs of the application programmers of customers, software companies, and IBM itself. Since he headed IBM's Software Development office in Milford, Connecticut, he had firsthand experience with the problems. He himself had a 10-year application's backlog and sought daily to trim that mountain. In addition, Steuri's sales and marketing organization could open doors to large customers who were willing to talk, and with Peter Dance's office in the red brick building across the street, it was easy to meet with Dance. As Software Marketing Manager, Dance was in daily contact with software companies; he could learn what they required. From this field and desk research, Saranga and his staff, in close cooperation with Wheeler, got a handle on the common applications interface and incorporated much of what they learned in the common user access, common programming, and common communications support efforts.

Application Enabling Tools

Saranga's second assignment was to manage the development of application enabling products to meet the common applications interface requirement. As head of IBM's Software Development, he supervised development of the Cross Systems Product (CSP), a language that enabled programmers to develop an application in one 370 environment and execute it in another. The CSP also enabled programmers to develop programs in the 8100 family (neither personal computer, 3X, nor 370) and execute them in the 370 environment.

Often it makes sense to develop an application in a particular hardware/software environment and execute or run the program in another. For example, highly productive programming languages and services may be available in one environment but not in another. Sometimes new applications are better developed off–line to avoid interfering with programs that are being executed. Even PC users who have installed a new application or reconfigured a system know how easy it is to bring a system down.

After developing the CSP for the 370 and 8100 families of computers, Saranga looked into the possibility of broadening its scope to encompass the PS/2 and the 3X families as well. If he could secure commitments from the product managers at the Cary, North Carolina, facility, IBM could say to software developers of the 370 line:

"Write your application on the SAA–supported CSP and you can execute it on all those hundreds of follow–on 3Xs and thousands of PS/2s you'll purchase." That would be very attractive to large customers. IBM could also say to software developers, for example: "Purchase the follow-on 3X, develop your next application on it using the CSP, and you'll be able to offer that software to the huge 370, 3X, and PS/2 customer base." Since the CSP was a highly productive language, IBM could also claim: "Write one line of CSP code for every four lines of COBOL or FORTRAN." Because of the strategic implications of the CSP, this was an important assignment.

IBM Applications

Saranga's third assignment also had strategic, long-term importance.

While IBM had attained moderate success in marketing applications software, some applications—like the Lockheed-developed Computer–Graphics Augmented Design and Manufacturing (CADAM)—were a huge success. CADAM gave IBM the largest share of the host- or mainframe-based computer-aided mechanical design market. It also established a solid and fairly unified base of users who would continue to purchase IBM software enhancements as well as additional hardware.

However, the proliferation of 370, 3X, and PC products resulted in a hodgepodge of IBM office software. Personal computer users, in fact, bought nearly every one except IBM's office tools and application software

packages. As a result, companies like Lotus that specialized in specific industries or applications solutions
were reaping the rewards of the growing office applications market. More importantly, there was no unified
base of office applications customers who could be
migrated to the next IBM product.

It was well known within IBM that the office market
for applications programming was huge, was growing,
and could form a solid base for future IBM software and
hardware sales. However, Saranga and Dance had not
been entirely successful in developing and marketing
office applications programs.

Wheeler and other IBM executives came upon an
idea that could change that situation and give the SAA
project a boost at the same time. The group suggested
that Saranga and Dance align their office applications
development and marketing strategy with the emerging SAA framework. Wheeler recommended that IBM
develop and market office applications common to the
three SAA-designated families of computers. This
would more sharply focus IBM's efforts to develop
application programs for the office and provide the
SAA tools to do it. It would also give Marketing a powerful competitive advantage.

Saranga and Dance now had a framework on which
to focus their efforts, and Wheeler got what he wanted—a lot of IBM software developers who would use
the SAA framework. He knew that an announcement
of IBM's plans to develop office applications conform-
ing to the SAA framework would convince a wary public, as well as some internal IBMers themselves, that
IBM and SAA were synonymous and that customers,
software developers, analysts, and everyone else in the

industry should begin to take SAA seriously.

In addition to reporting on any conflicts associated with the common applications interface and development of the Cross Systems Product, Saranga had to report on how he planned to handle the common applications for the office.

For the February 18 meeting, Saranga knew that he'd better have some straight answers for Earl Wheeler.

18 Saranga Makes a Hit

FEBRUARY 18, 1987—10:30 A.M.

Olive-complexioned Mike Saranga—jacket off and looking sharp in his powder-blue shirt—got up and stood by the projector. Casey may have liked yellow, but Mike apparently liked red. It was on every one of his transparencies.

Dick Hanrahan, Morris Taradalsky, and Don Casey all relaxed in their chairs. Al Atherton, Earl Wheeler's technical assistant, walked in and handed Wheeler a note. Wheeler paused to read it and then nodded to Al, who left the room. Someone else brought in a tray of coffee and Danish rolls.

Although Saranga formally reported to John Steuri, head of IIS, Wheeler exerted great influence over Saranga and his department's activities. It made sense—Steuri was busy trying to resurrect the computer services business; Wheeler had a few tricky things he wanted done; Saranga, with his broad technical experience (MVS operating system, the data bases IMS and DB2, and most recently applications programs) had the kind of background to get those things done. For more than a year, Saranga and his staff had been helping Wheeler piece together another aspect of what would become SAA.

Wheeler had invited Saranga to the February 18 meeting to report on the status of three different, but related, SAA projects. Saranga and three of his assistants —Allan Scherr, Tony Mondello, and Bob Berland—had worked hard to pull today's presentation together. Wheeler hoped that Saranga, the last of the four development executives to report, would not present any surprises—any conflicts that couldn't be resolved among the other three development VPs and the marketing representatives, Dance and Friedline, in the next hour or two. An important unresolved conflict could scratch the ten-minute trip to Old Orchard Road.

The most gregarious of the four developers, and as articulate as either Dance or Friedline, Mike Saranga began his presentation by saying that he had the cooperation of the other three development VPs in the room. However, three problem areas remained. If they could be resolved, the common application interface would be even more attractive to programmers.

The first problem area concerned the fact that two data communications subsystems, CICS/MVS and IMS/VS, had been omitted from SAA. Saranga pointed out that, to make life easy for programmers in all three environments, the PC, 3X, and 370 computers that access those subsystems needed to be part of SAA. He noted that Allan Scherr helped identify this need.

Scherr had completed a study of what was needed to create the desired applications environment; what Hanrahan, Taradalsky, and Casey agreed to develop went a long way toward improving the situation. However, Saranga told Wheeler and the group that the interfaces agreed to by the other development executives would do little to migrate applications from the 3X to the 370 families and to help customers who had IMS–based applications.

Several others, including Morris Taradalsky, agreed with Saranga's assessment. However, Casey was not ready to support additional communications interfaces. Here was an impasse—one that might keep them from presenting their plan to the Management Committee and announcing SAA.

After much discussion and collaboration, it was agreed that additional communication support was required, but not instantly. Casey agreed to give Dance the go ahead to announce enhancements to SAA communication support by October 1987. CICS/MVS and IMS/VS would be added to the SAA framework.

Cross Systems Product

Then Saranga addressed the status of the Cross Systems Product. He told the group that while getting the Cross Systems Product to support the three families was a bear of a project, Martha Rivers and others in Cary had agreed to support it across the three families.

Someone asked whether the PS/2 version of the Cross Systems Product would have a development ver-

sion as well as an execution version. Saranga replied
that his group didn't see an immediate need for a PS/2
development version, so only the execution version
would be made available. Apparently, Saranga's organization thought anyone who wanted to develop a 3X or
370 program should and would want to use either the
follow-on 3X or 370 products—not the PS/2—to do that.
However, if there were a real need for a Cross Systems
Product for PS/2 development, they would look at that
later. IBM developers can do anything, but they don't
always know exactly what to do at any given moment.

No unresolved conflict there. Saranga moved on to
his last topic.

Applications Development

Saranga reported that Tony Mondello had committed
to develop common applications. The initial SAA
announcement could include the clause: "It is IBM's
intent to develop common applications across the Systems Application Architecture environments."

At that moment, Wheeler realized that he had pulled
off the greatest coordination act in the history of IBM.
All four headstrong development VPs, representing
four divisions that not long ago hardly talked to each
other, had worked for the common good. They had
unequivocally committed themselves to the execution
of the Systems Application Architecture strategy. All
that remained was for Dance to discuss marketing
issues and for the group to go to the Management Committee for the final stamp of approval. They wouldn't

raise a red flag or postpone the show, now, would they? Not likely, but one never knows.

Wheeler let Saranga finish.

Saranga stated that the initial focus of applications development would be office applications and that later industry-specific applications would be added. Someone asked whether office applications would be available within two years. "Yeah."

Saranga explained that Tony Mondello and others had committed to have office applications available on the market within two years from the date of the initial announcement of SAA. Software would include programs for document creation, document library, personal services, mail, and decision support. He assured Wheeler that the managers were in the process of defining each other's projects.

These IBM-written applications would offer the same benefits of Systems Application Architecture as those written by other software vendors. IBM would offer consistency in how functions would be implemented, how panels would be laid out, and how the user would navigate within the application in all supported environments. Thus an application initially developed for one environment and subsequently ported to another would appear consistent to the application user. This consistency would also apply to integrated "families" of applications that would be offered.

Saranga went on to say that IBM intended to develop applications that conform to Systems Application Architecture, using common user access, common programming interface, and common communications support. These key applications would satisfy a significant customer need across the three Systems Application Architecture environments. They would help customers solve today's business problems in the most efficient way.

Recognizing the fact that software companies could view SAA as a competitive threat, someone in the group expressed concern about how the software vendors might react when IBM announced plans to develop office applications as part of SAA. A few minutes of discussion followed. Bob Berland (Saranga's assistant who represented IBM at ADAPSO—the professional association in which a large number of software companies were members) commented that some software companies specializing in office applications would have great concern about that; they would feel that they were being locked out of the market. But there were others who wouldn't take it seriously. Since IBM had failed in the past to market office applications for the PCs, they might assume that IBM would fail again. Berland progressed to the bigger issue of what the software industry would think about SAA in its entirety. He forecast that some would see it as an opportunity to use the standard pieces of software provided by SAA to develop customer applications more productively.

Berland also pointed out that with publications that define the IBM Systems Application Architecture and the availability of products, IBM would encourage software vendors and customers to develop applications based on its SAA products. He hoped that Friedline and Dance would be sure to get that message across to the software companies.

As Saranga's presentation ended, someone asked whether the Saint Patrick's Day kickoff was still on.

Wheeler smiled and looked at Peter Dance.

19 The Last, Dance

FEBRUARY 18, 1987—11:15 A.M.

Now it was Dance's turn. Smiling, he stood and walked toward Saranga.

Dance knew exactly why he was there. Six weeks earlier, he had given Wheeler the target date for the public launching of SAA. Today, Wheeler expected him to affirm that schedule and explain the details of the announcement.

As Wheeler waited for Dance to begin, he thought: Surely Dance would have alerted me or my assistant if he expected a delay in the schedule. He may have needed more time to pull things together. After all, the Information Systems Group had not actively pressed the development organizations to develop SAA. As a result, he may have been waiting for the right opportunity to exert the sales and marketing organization's clout.

Wheeler had at least three good reasons for wanting to announce SAA as soon as possible.

- First, he was ready. His Corporate Programming Department was ready. The four divisions represented by the four VPs who attended the morning meeting were ready. He knew that SAA concepts were well understood, the management structure was established, and the staffs of Corporate Programming and the four development organizations were in place.

- Second, IBM employees had to be briefed. As of the morning of February 18, relatively few people within IBM—those in the room, a handful of their staff, their immediate managers, the Management Committee, and a few others—knew anything about the SAA strategy. That left 99% or roughly 389,000 employees, who were unaware of the SAA strategy. Many of them would be needed to help execute the strategy. The sooner they were informed about the strategy, the sooner everyone would strive for consistency across the three product lines.

- Third, the customers, the press, and the rest of the industry had to be informed so they could take the actions that would make the SAA strategy a success.

Before today's meeting, very little had been said publicly about SAA. In an interview with *Computerworld* in January 1987, Ed Lucente, head of the U.S. sales and marketing organization, briefly referred to SAA. Then at the end of the first week in February, Allen Krowe, Group VP and member of the Management Committee, needing something encouraging to say at an IBM

Executive Forum, told 100 of IBM's largest customers that IBM was developing another architecture, the Systems Application Architecture, that would improve application portability. However, no *Computerworld* reader or Executive Forum attendee could have begun to imagine the scope of SAA, much less forseen how they should plan for it. The sooner customers and the software companies understood the features and benefits of SAA, the sooner they would take advantage of the emerging technology.

Wheeler probably had a fourth reason—one he would never reveal publicly. He had worked hard to encourage Saranga, Taradalsky, Hanrahan, and Casey, as well as their support teams, to claim SAA as their own. Yet SAA was Earl's Wheeler's creation. Providing the means for restructuring and resurrecting the greatest computer company in the world would be a monumental accomplishment. Earl Wheeler, like an anxious father, wanted his infant to take its first few steps toward that accomplishment.

Peter Dance had other motivations. He was anxious to mobilize the field sales and marketing organization. Training field salespeople on SAA would be a big task. Roughly 230,000 people were in the field, and not all were ready to absorb the concepts of SAA quickly. It could take months to train all of them. Also, at least 100,000 customer executives and executives from the 50 largest software companies had to be briefed. Lastly, several thousand journalists had to be informed about the user benefits of SAA. Clearly, these were gargantuan marketing tasks. Dance wanted to accomplish these objectives before 1987 ended. That was an important target.

Coach John Akers had called for a "hurry-up" offense on anything that could increase IBM's sales and profits. If Dance and his team moved fast, they could get it done.

Like Wheeler, Dance was driven by pride of owner- ship. His commitment was to introduce SAA as soon as possible to create an environment receptive to doing business with IBM.

Critical Timing

In previous discussions, all agreed that it would take until February 18 for the four development organiza- tions to sign off on the SAA requirements and for John Friedline and George Liptak to complete a good draft of the SAA marketing presentation materials. Then Lucente's field sales and marketing organization need- ed one month to prepare press releases, specification sheets, sales literature, speeches, and other marketing support materials. Add a month to February 18, and Wednesday, March 17—Saint Patrick's Day—would be the earliest possible announcement date.

If the announcement had to be postponed, the next suitable date would be early June because the announce- ment of the PS/2 personal computer had been sched- uled for April 2. Dance and his marketing colleagues believed that if SAA were announced after March 17 but before April 2, the SAA would be subordinated by the excitement of the impending PS/2 announcement and go unnoticed for at least 30 days.

Another possibility was to delay the PS/2 announce- ment for a few days or a week or two. That would give

the sales and marketing organization more time to prepare the SAA announcement. However, this was never
seriously considered. Wheeler and Dance both believed
that SAA would have much greater long-term significance to IBM than the PS/2. SAA held the promise of
generating hundreds of billions of computer sales
while saving billions of dollars in R&D expenditures.
But it would be a few years before IBM could reap the
benefits of SAA. IBM's balance sheet had to be
improved *now*. IBM's sales and earnings for the calendar year 1987 were meager. The PS/2 could help add a
few billion to the financial statement. Needing short-
term results, Wheeler and Dance knew they had to proceed with the announcement of the PS/2.

Once they realized that March 17 was the only suitable day for the SAA announcement, Dance promised
that the sales and marketing organization would somehow get everything done on time. Then Dance suggested a way in which they could use the PS/2 announcement to their advantage. They could ask Hanrahan to
link the PS/2 to the SAA in his announcement. Wheeler and Dance agreed to link SAA to all future product
announcements.

Dance Reports

When Peter Dance revealed that the field was ready to
announce Systems Application Architecture on Saint
Patrick's Day, Wednesday, March 17, everyone applaud-
ed. Dance beamed. Wheeler heard what he wanted and
expected to hear. If Dance had said ISG could not meet
that date, Wheeler would have asked Dance to explain.

Wheeler would not have accepted a delay unless Akers, Kuehler, or Krowe had approved it. Fortunately, the schedule was on target.

Field Briefing

Wheeler wanted to know how his offspring would be announced to the world. Dance told him that two weeks before the announcement, each branch office would receive an invitation to send one or two of its support personnel to Atlanta, Georgia, for a two-day briefing on SAA. He expected 150 members of the Information Systems Group to be there. The program would start at 11:30 A.M. on Monday, March 15, two days before the public announcement. The briefing would end at 3:00 P.M. on Tuesday, March 16. An 11:30 A.M. start time would allow at least those on the East Coast and even some attendees west of Atlanta to arrive that day rather than the night before. A 3:00 P.M. conclusion should allow everyone to return home at a reasonable time on Tuesday. By Wednesday, everyone would be ready to brief their colleagues on SAA.

Dance would begin the briefing with an overview, stressing that SAA was no ordinary announcement. Jim Henderson, one of Dance's managers, would then review the market development resources being mobilized to support the strategy. John Friedline would give an in-depth presentation of SAA. Following Friedline, one member of each of the four development organizations would give a technical presentation of each of the four SAA layers. Finally, Jim Henderson would close the session.

Someone wanted to know where the briefing would be held. Dance responded that he had reserved the auditorium in Building A on the fourth floor of the old General Systems Division's headquarters (now called the Lake Shore building).

Someone else wanted to know the names of the four speakers from the development organizations.

Dance said that each of the four development VPs would select a speaker. Taradalsky said he would send Carol Schira. The other three had not made an assignment yet.

Dance concluded by stating that this briefing should prepare the field to respond to customer inquiries on SAA.

Public Briefing

Dick Hanrahan then asked how the public announcement would be handled. Development executives like to know these things.

Dance told the group that Corporate Marketing and the field sales and marketing organization had agreed to use 590 Madison Avenue, New York, for the public announcement on March 17. This location was selected because IBM's most strategic announcements are always made there, and the press knows it. Making the announcement from this location should send a signal to the press, the financial analysts, and the consulting community that SAA was considered extremely important and should be covered that way.

Saranga asked who would make the announcement. Dance explained that he would leave for New York after the Atlanta briefing to tie down the loose ends for Wednesday's announcement. Larry Ford, Dance's boss, would kick off the conference; then Dance would embellish on Ford's opening remarks. A few other executives would also participate, but none had been selected yet.

Someone said that Earl should be there. Wheeler shook his head in disagreement. Facing the press members seated in the red upholstered seats at 590 Madison, the flashes of cameras, the voice amplification over the microphone, the elevated podium—these were the domain of the marketing people. It's not for IBM developers, not even for the VP of Corporate Programming. Besides, he needed to concentrate, not on speaking but on directing the developers.

Wheeler asked what approach Dance would take in explaining SAA to the press. With that, the Kentuckian began to blush. Dance's face always turns red when he gets nervous, and it was still too early for him to feel comfortable articulating the features and benefits of Systems Application Architecture. He was understandably nervous.

Dance told the group that he was not sure exactly how he would pitch SAA. As he said that, he started to flip through the slides that John Friedline had given him an hour or so ago.

He said he might start out saying:

> Today, IBM announces its Systems Application Architecture, a collection of selected software interfaces, conventions, and protocols that will be published in 1987. IBM's SAA will be the framework for developing consistent applications across future offerings of

the major IBM computing environments
—System/370, System/3X, and Personal Computer.

He and everyone in the room liked the sound of
that. Dance started to relax.

Then he said he might say something like:

What IBM Corporation is announcing today
is not a product. It is important to understand that SAA is not a product. You can't go
out and buy it—it is not in place yet—it is a
journey we've just begun. It is a long-term
direction of significance to IBM customers.

He again paused. The attendees liked the sound of
that, too. Smiling, Dance was pleased with himself.

He then added that SAA consists of four related elements: (1) common user access, (2) common programming interface, (3) common communications support,
and (4) common applications (which will be developed,
adhering to the standards established for the first three).
As he said that, he placed one of John Friedline's slides
on the overhead projector. The slide looked very much
like Figure 1.

◆ Common User Access (CUA)

◆ Common Programming Interface (CPI)

◆ Common Communications Support (CCS)

◆ Common Applications

Figure 1 – Four Elements of Systems Application Architecture

After adjusting the slide a bit, he said that SAA is too complex to define in a half-hour session. Neither the press nor anyone else could be expected to absorb its scope and importance. He would be happy if he merely alerted the press about SAA.

Then he pointed to the first bullet on the slide and said the common user access will be designed for the user and optimized by the particular workstation. Hanrahan started to say that a good part of it is based on the Presentation Manager, but then stopped.

Then Dance pointed to second bullet and said the common programming interface would include an assortment of important languages—"common" higher-level languages, an application generator, a procedures language, and a 5GL (fifth generation language) —and an assortment of services consisting of a data base interface, a query interface, a presentation and dialog interface, and distributed services. Taradalsky and Schira listened carefully as Dance mentioned the common programming interface.

Taradalsky interrupted, pointing out the need to stress that the operating systems supported are the MVS, 3X follow-on, and OS/2. "We should not mislead the public into thinking that IBM will support all the operating systems." Dance agreed.

Then Dance pointed to the next item and said:

> Common communications support will consist of extensions to existing communications architectures. It will be based on SNA and "selected" international standards, will support distributed functions, and will be consistent with open communications architecture.

Don Casey smiled and nodded his head in agreement.

As he spoke about the elements of Systems Application Architecture, Dance showed a second slide, which looked roughly like Figure 2.

At this point, Dance said that it is the combination of the three elements that makes common applications possible. Those three elements—the common user access, the common programming interface, and the common communications support—will make it possible for customers to implement and use IBM computers more effectively. When he gave the presentation at 590 Madison Avenue, he planned to state:

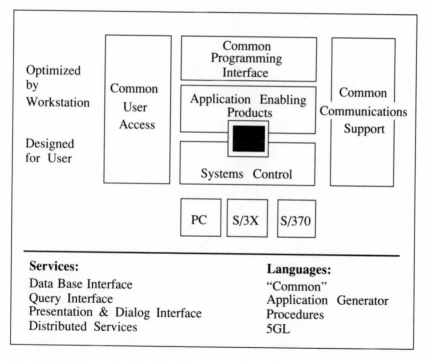

Figure 2 – Systems Application Architecture

"IBM's Systems Application Architecture is a
set of software interfaces, conventions, and
protocols—a framework for productively
designing and developing applications with
cross–system consistency. SAA defines the
foundation for building portable, consistent
application systems for the future."

Saranga, who had been quieter than normal, added
that another point must be made: "SAA defines the
foundation upon which portable, consistent applications can be built in the future, *provided* that you use
IBM hardware, control programs, and IBM Systems
Application Architecture products." Dance had no comment.

Then Bob Berland, one of Mike Saranga's assistants,
suggested that Dance not limit himself. He should tell
them: "If they are developing applications programs
and/or systems and if they observe these interfaces, conventions, and protocols, they are being assured by IBM
that future IBM hardware–software products will conform to these."

Dance responded: "Bob's comment brings up a good
point. The press should be told that during 1987, IBM
will publish documentation on recommended interfaces, conventions, and protocols that will be supported
by *future* IBM hardware–software products that will
enable the development of consistent applications
across the System/370, System/3X, and Personal Computer architectures."

As Dance was winding down what was less a presentation than a group discussion, just about everyone in
the room agreed that Systems Application Architecture

would be difficult to explain, not only to the press but to everyone else as well. Even IBM employees would have difficulty understanding SAA.

Then Dance said, as he returned to his seat, that he was thinking about saying that Systems Application Architecture may be at least as important as the announcement of OS/360 in the 1960s and SNA in the 1970s. He continued: "Systems Application Architecture probably represents the most challenging systems commitment that has ever been undertaken."

After he said that, there was silence. Everyone just sat there for a moment. The development executives realized that they were working on the creation of something so important that it had to be compared to IBM's two greatest accomplishments! They all knew that each and every one of them played a part in creating what might become one of IBM's greatest achievements.

Wheeler spoke up. He told the group that they had not arrived yet—they still needed to head over to the Management Committee and present to them. He had their attention. They all knew they had to get the nod from the MC before orders could be disseminated throughout the IBM organization to mobilize resources behind the SAA.

At that point, Al Atherton said that the MC was expecting Wheeler, the four development executives, and Dance at 1:30. Atherton suggested that they meet outside the MC room at 1:15. With that, the first meeting ended.

20 As the World Turns

FEBRUARY 18, 1987

Purchase, New York—11:45 A.M. EST

Dick Hanrahan, Don Casey, Morris Taradalsky, Mike Saranga and others attending the meeting stood up. Some headed for the facilities, the cafeteria, or the phones—depending on their needs. Others paired off to discuss the meeting and SAA-related topics. All of them felt good about what had happened—the first hurdle had been leaped successfully.

For a little over a year, this group had worked toward the day when they could go to the MC and tell them they had a plan to attack the problems customers faced in implementing and using computers—problems that kept customers from buying computers. The VPs of four different divisions and a marketing executive had all agreed on what was to be developed and initially offered to customers.

Dick Hanrahan had agreed to develop the Presentation Manager as the cornerstone of Wheeler's plan to develop a common user interface across all three products.

Morris Taradalsky would support the development of a set of programs and services that would be common across all three hardware families.

Saranga promised to have the Cross System Product software available not just for 370 MVS and VM programmers, but for those in the 3X follow-on and PS/2 environments. Similarly, Casey and Dance were committed to their parts of the endeavor.

But was Wheeler's, the four VPs', and Dance's agreement that they were ready to announce SAA enough? No. Other questions and approval remained. How would the Management Committee react to what Wheeler and the rest of the team agreed to do? Could the MC discover a flaw in the plan? Might the MC decide not to let them go ahead with the plan until they made major changes? The next major hurdle—the afternoon meeting—would provide the answers.

Armonk, New York—11:45 A.M. EST

Ten minutes away from Earl Wheeler's office, John Akers looked to his right, then to his left, and asked the other members of the committee whether they wanted to break. The consensus was yes.

In the Armonk atrium among the ficus bushes, Carl Crawford paced, waiting for a cab to the airport. He felt

25 pounds lighter and 10 years younger. He thought the presentation went well. It had taken him 25 minutes to present the current usage of such terms as *cooperative, dispersed, distributed,* and *enterprise processing.*

Upstairs in the conference room, some of the Management Committee members had already begun to leave. Two lingered behind. One said, "That was quite a day yesterday." The other looked up and said, "What, Jack's press conference?"

"No, I meant the market."

"Oh, it sure was. The Dow climbed 54.14 points to finish at 2,237.49, an all–time record."

"Yeah, we closed around $117. That's not bad."

"Sure hope we don't get clobbered too much in the market correction."

"Me, too."

"Did you hear what Gates did yesterday?

"Bill Gates—the Microsoft guy who's providing the basic version of the PS/2 operating system?"

"No, I meant Robert M. Gates, Reagan's nominee to head the CIA. He testified yesterday that he would probably have recommended against sending weapons to Iran if he'd been CIA director."

Montvale, New Jersey—11:45 A.M. EST

At Hanrahan's division headquarters, IBM executives were starting to think about lunch. Some wondered what would happen at this afternoon's session. Several IBMers thought they knew.

On the other side of the building, the fellow seeking "Akers Edge" never even thought about Hanrahan's meeting with the big and powerful in Purchase and Armonk today.

Outside, the sky cleared a little.

Milford, Connecticut—11:45 A.M. EST

At Mike Saranga's and Peter Dance's offices in Milford, Connecticut, three men who worked for them headed downtown for a New England lunch at the Saybrook Fish House on Broad Street. As they headed for a car one of them said, "I'm convinced we're finished. We'll never do it again."

Another said, "You're crazy. Next year we'll clobber the competition again."

They were discussing football. Just three weeks earlier, their team—the New York Giants—had for the first time since they could remember, won the Super Bowl, trouncing Denver 39 to 20. They would continue to rave about the Giants' success for some time.

Raleigh, North Carolina—11:45 A.M. EST

Avery Upchurch backed his car down the icy hill near his home until the incline bottomed out and then continued backing up the next incline. Thirty yards up that hill, he brought the car to a stop. Avery Upchurch, Raleigh's Mayor, said to himself, "I've got to make it. I don't know how many times I've tried this, but I've got to get up that hill. I've got to get into town before that meeting ends." The City Council was meeting to decide what they should do next to restore city services. Upchurch wanted to be there.

The secondary road Upchurch lived on was covered with ice and snow. To get onto a main artery and head for town, he had to make it up the hill. To do so, he needed a running start.

Upchurch put the car in first, slowly let up on the clutch and gently pressed the gas pedal. The car rolled forward down the first hill gaining momentum toward the bottom, which drove it up the second hill. Skidding and crunching, a sweating, struggling, praying Avery Upchurch made it! An hour or so later he would attend the meeting.

Dr. Ed Sussenguth and Paul Lindfors of SNA fame thought about going out and shoveling some of the ice and snow that covered their front walks, but dismissed the idea. Raleigh was a mess. Bill Warner, Don Heile, and Vann Hettinger, assistants to Don Casey, wouldn't mash any elevator buttons today, but the latest weather reports indicated that the worst of the storm was over.

San Jose, California—8:45 A.M. PST

It was three hours earlier in San Jose than in Purchase, Armonk, Montvale, Milford, or Raleigh. Taradalsky's secretary, Anita, logged on to PROFS to check the morning messages. Jnon Dash, who had just returned from the assignment of helping Austin, Texas, implement the relational Data Manager, and Ed Lassettre sipped coffee as they walked in the Santa Teresa courtyard.

"Morris tell you he's meeting with Wheeler and the MC this afternoon?

"No."

"Well, I heard he is."

21 The Architect

After his conference concluded, Earl Wheeler, who apportions his time wisely, spent no more than 10 minutes tying up a few loose ends. Small talk was a luxury he could ill afford. Satisfied with the outcome of this meeting, he excused himself, grabbed a sandwich, and returned to his office to review his morning mail and to prepare for that afternoon's meeting with the Management Committee.

Surely the MC must have known that the Systems Application Architecture plan devised by Wheeler and the four development VPs would encompass the most sweeping and grandiose undertaking the computer industry had ever seen. They planned to impose a structure, four layers deep—user interface, applications, application enabling, and communications—across multiple operating system and hardware environments. Just creating the structure, much less fitting all of IBM's straggling mainline software and hardware product lines into that structure, represented an awesome undertaking.

Leaders like Wheeler are rare these days. What's he like? How did he get to be that way? How did he get the other's to go along with him?

Earl Wheeler did not just arrive one day at the IBM Corporate Headquarters fully equipped with the broad, and in-depth knowledge needed to create the four-layer structure of SAA, to apply it across IBM's four operating systems and three hardware environments, and to motivate people to get the job done. He evolved.

School Days

Earl Wheeler graduated with an engineering degree from Union College, a relatively exclusive, private, four-year liberal arts and engineering school with fewer than 2000 students, 10 miles west of Albany, New York, and the Hudson River. He belonged to the Delta Phi fraternity and Air Force ROTC.

Wheeler joined IBM as a junior engineer in 1955 and was assigned to the Endicott Laboratory. Fresh from college, he could not have known much about computers or software except what IBM's training program taught him. In those days, computers for institutional purposes were almost non-existent.

As an electrical engineering student Wheeler learned much about the characteristics of electrons and how resistors, capacitors, and especially vacuum tubes magnify, shape, and otherwise control the flow of electricity. But Wheeler probably never saw a transistor, except in a research paper, or built a transistor based on a flip–flop circuit, until after he graduated, since the transistor had been invented only four years before he entered Union College. Transistors came into general use in computers in 1960, five years after Wheeler had graduated. As the technology grew—from transistors to integrated circuits to large-scale integrated circuits and then to very large-scale integrated circuits—so did Wheeler's knowledge of the industry and the applications.

In college, Wheeler not only learned to be an engineer, but he also adopted an attitude that prevails today. Union College admonishes that "every student should learn to gather and evaluate information, to think coherently, to write succinctly, to form aesthetic judgments, and to view a time and place from a perspective of knowledge." Wheeler's actions at IBM have consistently demonstrated a passion for doing just that. To have developed the SAA strategy attests to those beliefs. Had he not gathered and evaluated huge amounts of information about IBM's products and people; had he not striven to put the disparate elements together logically; had he not viewed the needs of the users and software developers of each of the different hardware and software environments from the perspective of knowledge, he could not have created the SAA strategy. Without such an approach, taming the jungle of IBM hardware and software products would have been a super-Herculean undertaking. Wheeler had, indeed, learned his lessons well.

Uncle Sam Beckons

When Earl Wheeler took the IBM job in Endicott, he had no idea it would last only a few months. No, he was not promoted. Instead, he switched to another employer—not a fledgling computer company, but the U.S. Government. Wheeler stored his first business suit in the closet and put on a blue Air Force uniform to perform the service required by his ROTC scholarship. In two years the Air Force would help him on the way to being "all that he could be."

The Air Force, which owned Univacs and some IBM 700 Series unit record computers, needed bright, detail-oriented, logical, open-minded people who understood algorithms and could make those computers do something useful. Young Wheeler had those attributes, so the Air Force assigned him to programming computers. For two years, at the dawn of computing, Wheeler mastered the fundamental concepts of programming and the use of at least two different machine languages. This experience had to influence his career path.

The Air Force did more than develop Wheeler the programmer. The two years of duty coupled with his ROTC training at Union College helped develop Wheeler the strategist. Earl Wheeler's SAA strategy heeds Napoleon's words of wisdom: "Go separately but hit in unison—that is the greatest art of strategy." One can easily envision the long reach of Wheeler's mind directing four powerful IBM armies—Saranga's application developers, Taradalsky's Santa Teresa Labs programmers, Hanrahan's personal computing developers, and Casey's communications programmers—to go separately toward the objectives set by their division presidents while instructing them where and when to come together and hit in unison.

A knowledge of strategic concepts would later enable Wheeler to convince a group of IBM operating system product managers to become part of the SAA undertaking. He got the MVS and VM people on board and then pursued the OS/2 people before he approached the developers of the operating system for the 3X follow-on. Although he says he did not apply a "double pincer" to get the 3X people committed, mere use of that term indicates that he understood the application of resources through frontal attacks, envelopments, pincers, and other military strategems. Like Union College, the Air Force prepared him well.

Endicott Days

After his discharge from the Air Force in 1957, Wheeler returned to IBM and the Philadelphia branch. He continued to work there for two years. Former IBM employees like Buck Rogers, author of *The IBM Way*, and others have written about IBM's culture. Many readers already have their own opinion of that culture and can form their own judgments of how it contributed to shaping Earl Wheeler.

After two years at IBM, a major opportunity emerged deep in upstate New York in a little town 60 or so miles southwest of Union College. IBM needed programmers at its Endicott facility to design an operating system for a computer it was developing. This computer—the S/360 processor—would provide the product that IBM needed to emerge as the world's dominant computer manufacturer. When Earl Wheeler accepted the job at Endicott, perhaps it was the opportunity to get back into programming, which he enjoyed in the Air Force; to become involved in the embryonic stage of S/360 systems software development; to return to his home state; to get out of a field office that provided limited growth potential; to work in a development center where the action appealed to a technically oriented person; or perhaps he just did not like Philadelphia—any or all of these reasons may have influenced him.

In 1960, lanky Earl Wheeler walked into the IBM Endicott Glendale Laboratory and became a systems programmer. For nearly 10 years, except for a short assignment elsewhere, Wheeler worked in Endicott. From managing groups of programmers and engineers, he eventually rose to the position of Systems Manager, Intermediate Systems. In those days an intermediate system encompassed the Systems 360/25, 360/30, and the emerging 370 models.

In the first year or two at Endicott, Wheeler acquired a good understanding of one of the S/360 models. As soon as he began to work on other S/360 models and the S/370, however, he undoubtedly began to appreciate the importance of a system's architecture. Working on different computers had to make him appreciate the importance of structure and the differences and similarities among various structures. One does not often get to manage a major computer development project unless one appreciates the structure on which the system is built.

Wheeler the manager began to emerge at Endicott. There he probably learned not to give orders and expect subordinates to follow them blindly, but to ask them to get something done and encourage alternative ideas. It would take several more years before he would take the time to explain what had to be done; to get agreement that the problem needed fixing; to ask how it should be done; to propose his own solution if he did not like what he heard; and to say, "If you don't like the plan I proposed; present a better one."

Kingston Lab

In May of 1970, Wheeler was transferred and promoted to Director of IBM's Kingston Lab, where major activities included large systems software for the Kingston programming center, development activities that would result in the 3270 display terminal, some work in power systems, and special engineering.

In the sixties, the Kingston Lab had been a hotbed of big processors, time-shared systems, display systems, and special systems for space and military applications. Briefly, in 1964, Kingston Lab was responsible for the larger S/360, Models 65, 67, and 75; in 1966 it built the IBM 2250 used for the Gemini flight simulator; in 1966 it built the air traffic control system delivered to the FAA in Atlantic City; in May 1967 it shipped the first S/360 Model 67 (time sharing) to M.I.T.; in January 1968 it announced the S/360 Model 86; in 1969 it developed a new control method for data processing used for the Apollo 11 mission.

When Wheeler joined the Kingston Lab, extensive activity was underway to develop the 3270 display terminal as a replacement for the 2260 and to develop communications controllers for the IBM product line. Meanwhile, concepts and plans for Systems Network Architecture were being formulated by Sussenguth and Lindfors at IBM's Raleigh Lab. Wheeler's mission in Kingston, to a good extent, was to try to adapt Kingston's communication-based products to Raleigh's SNA structure. Communications technology played a major role in the Kingston environment. There Wheeler gained valuable experience working with large, complex systems and acquired an appreciation of their communications requirements. Through this experience, Wheeler not only understood the difficulty of fitting something into an existing structure or architecture, but he also observed how the SNA people went about solving problems. He would subsequently adapt Raleigh's approach and go one better.

His earlier 370 experience in Endicott coupled with the experience he was now getting in the communications area gave him the push he needed to scale the IBM corporate ladder quickly. In a few short years, this project started him on the path to developing some key concepts needed for SAA.

In May 1971, IBM announced Kingston's 3270 Information Display System. IBM would sell several millions of these computer terminals. Other manufacturers would build hundreds of thousands of 3270-compatible terminals, making the system an important industry standard. People around the world would learn to use the 3270 displays and keyboards to interface with IBM 370 mainframes. This experience showed Wheeler the importance of the investment that customers made in training their staff to utilize that particular computer–user interface.

Wheeler also managed the development of other important communications products including the VTAM (Virtual Terminal Access Method) communications software system that enabled terminals to more easily access mainframe software, and the IBM 3790 communication system. VTAM was announced in June 1973, and in December 1973, Wheeler had a new assignment. During his Kingston stay, however, Wheeler increased his knowledge of the communications issues facing the users as well as that of IBM's emerging communications technology. His next assignment would provide him with another set of important experiences and boost him to the rank of vice president.

1972—VP Industry Systems Division

In 1972 IBM created the Systems Development Division and Systems Products Division. Earl Wheeler was named VP of Industry Systems in the Systems Development Division. Roughly 17 years after graduating from Union College, Earl Wheeler was VP of a good-sized operation.

At this point in IBM's development, the company had great interest in developing systems to meet the specific needs of particular industry sectors, such as banking, insurance and retail. As VP, Wheeler attempted to understand the application requirements of customers and to develop industry-specific systems to meet those requirements. One example of his efforts is the highly successful IBM 3600 Finance Communications System for the banking industry. That product was not announced until 1973, and over the years, great numbers of banks have used the system.

This experience led him to understand customer needs more than ever before in his IBM career. Besides gaining knowledge of the application requirements of different industries, he learned that although the sys-

tems he had been helping to build were important, providing customers with solutions to their specific application requirements mattered most. Perhaps this is why
Wheeler wanted a highly experienced development executive—Mike Saranga—to concentrate on the common applications aspect in the development of SAA.
Moreover, by helping to develop industry systems,
Wheeler had a good opportunity to understand the
challenge of developing transaction-processing systems
—systems that customers used to run their business: to
process debits and credits, sell or purchase stock, and increase or decrease inventory items. This experience had
to make him aware of the importance of data base management systems, such as IMS, that were being developed in Santa Teresa at that time. This knowledge of
transaction processing requirements and of the limita-
tions of a data base like IMS helped him to decide quickly that SAA would be based on relational data base technology.

By the early seventies, Wheeler had already gained a
strong horizontal perspective of computer systems development. Managing several products in the 360 and
370 families required that he think horizontally across
those product lines. As a result, he acquired a horizontal perspective of IBM products while his peers focused
on software that was stacked on top of products in his
realm. The Industry Systems assignment required that
he think vertically. He had to think about what software would be stacked on top of the basic hardware plat-
form as he tried to create industry, or vertical,
solutions. At this point, IBM had developed an executive with both qualities of thinking.

1975—VP Communications Systems Division

In 1975, Wheeler again had an opportunity not only to strengthen his ability to think horizontally across the 370 product line, but to master his understanding of IBM's emerging communications technology and to learn some key aspects of managing a major development effort. In that year he was named VP of the Communications Systems Division in Kingston, New York.

Wheeler's primary mission as VP of the Communications Systems Division was to drive SNA across the Kingston, Raleigh, and LaGaude development environments, and to make sure that these divisions worked together to make the SNA architecture a reality. This, of course, added to his storehouse of valuable experience. Having to implement the SNA structure across the Kingston development organization gave him first-hand experience of what it was like to be structured. And it gave him the opportunity to see how the SNA people drove SNA across not just his operation, but the entire company.

SNA's developers held regular meetings for product managers throughout the company. At these meetings, they motivated the managers to modify their designs to conform to SNA by pointing out that, for the common good, it was necessary for them to give a little in their design plans. If that did not work, product managers were told that for their own good, plans had to conform, otherwise their product would not interconnect with the mainline IBM products. Inability to connect would lead to the products' failure in the marketplace. If that argument didn't work, Sussenguth and Lindfors

would ask their superior to exert a different kind of
pressure.

When Wheeler initiated his own SAA meetings, he
added a devastating twist, one that would make it
unlikely for higher ups in the IBM Corporation ever to
be called on to apply additional pressure. He attended
each meeting himself. Not only was his power of per-
suasion excellent, but people wanted to be there just
because he was there. Wheeler didn't need superiors to
exert pressure.

Wheeler makes mistakes, too, just like the rest of us.
One of Wheeler's biggest and most noticeable failures
concerned the 8100 Information System, announced on
October 3, 1978. That product was intended to be used as
a cluster controller for the 3270 terminals so IBM customers could distribute some processing off the mainframe and develop distributed processing applications.

Wheeler thought the 8100 was a good product.
Unlike many other products, the software structure of
the 8100 was excellent and conformed to a well-thought-
out, layered structure, which should have made it possible to easily upgrade or otherwise modify the software.
The market disagreed. The product bombed as badly as
the PCjr did.

The product bombed for several reasons. Wheeler
has said, "I think one of the reasons that we didn't get
the acceptance that I wanted was because the interfaces
weren't consistent with the 370." Many people agree.
Wheeler added, "And I can learn not only from my success, but also from my failures. Look at the interfaces of
SAA and you will see how I learned from my mistakes." SAA includes interfaces for all the growth and

mainline software products of the 370 as well as for the other two mainline hardware environments.

1978-1980—Westchester

In 1978, Wheeler took a very meaningful lateral move when he was named Group Director of Systems Development reporting to Jack Kuehler, Assistant Group Executive, Information Systems and Technology Group. When Kuehler moved on in 1980, Wheeler assumed his position. As Group Director, Wheeler was responsible for developing the strategy for software for S/370 systems, which would become IBM's most important computer family. Few people suspected that shortly after he started that job, he began to execute actions that would lead to the announcement of SAA years later. Wheeler himself did not know where the road would lead.

Before Wheeler took over, it seems IBM had difficulty managing the development of the 370 MVS software products. The software development effort had been spread among facilities in Poughkeepsie, Raleigh, Santa Teresa, and Hursley, jeopardizing management control. More important, the development progressed in such a way that an almost random assortment of software modules performed the function of a single software product. One software product manager would develop his product using a line of communications software, say C1; add a language L1; and write the sort S1 to produce a software product called Random 1. Another product manager would use a communications mod-

ule C5, perhaps the same language L1, a different sort
module S9, and yield a product called Random 2. IBM
management must have felt as Luke Skywalker did
when he walked into that Star Wars bar and saw mutations with no discernible pattern or classification.

With the hodgepodge of software products, Earl
Wheeler could not view MVS software development
as a whole or total system. As a result, the odds were
good that he could not position MVS software development in time and place. Therefore, he could not develop a strategy to advance MVS software until this problem was corrected.

Structuring

After a few months on the job, Wheeler realized that
the key to solving the problem was to study the software mutations and to develop a structure that would
bring order out of chaos. He reasoned that if he could fit
MVS products into a structure, he would see the totali-
ty of the MVS software and its position in time and
place. He could then develop the 370 software strategy.

After considerable thought, he and his staff developed the four-layer structure shown in Figure 1. Starting at the bottom, the layers consisted of (1) systems
control, which is closest to the hardware, (2) a communications layer that enabled one program to communicate with another, (3) an application enabling layer,
which consisted of the languages and data base management systems, and (4) applications.

The four-layer structure enabled Wheeler to look at
the different pieces of software that made up a major

software program and to classify the pieces into one of four categories or layers, based on the function of the software module and its synergistic relationship to other pieces of software. For example, the communications programs VTAM and NCP (Network Control Program) fit into the communications layer. All languages such as COBOL and FORTRAN as well as data base management systems such as IMS and DB2 fit into the application enabling layer. The MVS operating control programs fell in the systems control layer. Since the developers were not doing much with applications, nothing fit into the applications layer.

This breakthrough structure held the promise of untangling all important MVS programs that had been developed. The structure would also help assure that all future MVS software would be developed within this framework. This approach would greatly improve productivity. Imagine how much easier it would be for

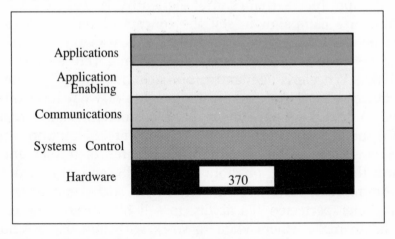

Figure 1 – 370 Cross System Layered Software, 1982

the IBM software developers if, when they needed an application enabling program or a communications program, they could find it listed under the MVS applications enabling layer or communications layer instead of within some other program. The discovery of this structure formed the basis for the SAA developments that followed. It was Wheeler's first concrete step toward SAA.

Wheeler still faced the challenge of getting the 370 MVS software development organizations to implement the four-layer structure. Wheeler would not be denied. In answering this challenge, he perfected his salesmanship and principles of strategy.

Salesmanship

Since Wheeler held a staff position as Assistant Group Executive, he had no direct authority over MVS software product activities. Consequently, Wheeler had to launch a campaign to sell the concept of the four-layer structure to key IBM executives. This was the purpose of his visit to Mike Saranga at the Santa Teresa Labs in 1980. Wheeler's general approach in these circumstances was (1) to explain the benefits of what he wanted to do, (2) get agreement that the problem existed, and (3) obtain commitment to implement a solution. In Saranga's case, he explained the benefits of implementing this structure, possibly on the IMS, and obtained a commitment from him. Through such encounters, Wheeler perfected his ability to sell his ideas to others and to make others want to work with him. He would use that skill throughout his career.

Strategy

While perfecting his selling ability, Wheeler also practiced the principles of strategy. When one product manager agreed to conform to the structure and cooperate with him, in effect, an alliance was formed. Wheeler would then visit another product manager and mention that he had the support of the first manager. In doing so, Wheeler practiced a principle of alliance: *Form alliances where you are weak to attain your goals.* Wheeler formed alliances with everyone he could until he gained strength everywhere.

When he and half a dozen supporters unexpectedly walked into the office of a product manager who needed convincing, he practiced a principle of surprise: *Use the element of the unexpected to magnify the force applied.*

By the end of 1981, MVS software could be viewed as an entity, the development process was being managed more effectively, and productivity gains were appearing. Wheeler then applied a principle of strategy to tame the other two bodies of 370 software, the VM– and VSE–based jungles of software. Here he applied the principle of momentum: *Use the element of your momentum to immediately seize another objective.* His success in taming MVS software suddenly gave him a boost in momentum. He used that thrust to attain quick agreement from the VM and VSE software managers.

Software Interface

By late 1982, all 370 departmental systems conformed structurally to the four-layer concept. Developers could look across the layers and see a consistent view of software products across three operating systems (see Figure 2).

Once developers could view software products across the layers, they realized that the points where the software layer intersected a particular operating system represented a "design point." Wheeler and his developers used the concept of design points to decide where software should or should not be developed. For example, they were able to focus management attention on the application enabling/MVS design point or the communications/VM design point and say: "What is happening at this specific design point? Do we have a hole there? Fill it. We have three efforts to develop software for that specific design point? Kill two of them."

Then Wheeler made an important discovery. He discovered that the design points, where the layers inter-

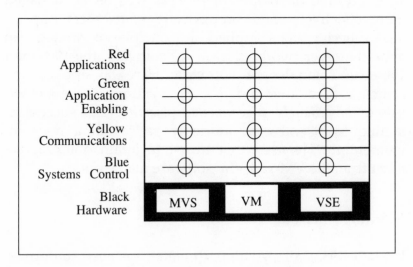

Figure 2 – Design Points across Three Operating Systems

sected the operating system, also flagged the "software interface points" of all IBM 370 software. The design points were not just design points, but software interface points.

There was the key concept IBM needed to develop "cooperative" and "enterprise" systems, to develop interconnected 370, 3X, and PS/2 solutions. The software interface points show where the systems interconnect with each other. Develop consistent software interfaces and you have interconnected systems. The discovery that the design points were also software interface points provided the insights that Wheeler needed to see how it would be possible for IBM to go for the whole enchilada—four consistent layers of interfaces across three discrete operating environments. Consistent software interfaces could make that possible. If IBM could manage those interfaces, they would, in time, create a body of consistent interfaces.

Once Wheeler saw how valuable the concepts of design points and software interface points were to the software development decision-making process, he was convinced that managing software by the layers was the correct approach to a multiple operating system environment. If being able to focus management attention on decisive points and issues is half the challenge of management, then Wheeler accomplished that half with his approach to managing by layers.

Bringing Some Color into the Picture

In the early eighties, Wheeler and his associates faced increasing difficulty in explaining the interconnection concepts to others in the company, much less themselves. To make their presentations more effective, they assigned a color to each of the layers: blue for system control, yellow for communications, green for applications enabling, and red for applications. The group working on systems control programs became known as the Blue Team, the Green Team, and so on. Casey headed up the Yellow Team. When the user interface layer was added, it was assigned the color purple.

1984—Programming Director, Corporate Headquarters

In 1984, top management at IBM—recognizing the importance of integrating software across three product lines—decided that Earl Wheeler had spent enough time focusing on the 370. Members of the Management Committee thought it just might be a good idea if they put Wheeler in a position where he could also focus on midrange and PC software development. As Director of Programming, Wheeler's task was to convince the PS/2 developers that they needed structuring next. This decision might at first seem illogical, since the midrange 3X follow-on preceded the PS/2 in the hierarchy of products. Surely, you would expect that after structuring the 370, Wheeler would next attempt to structure the 3X follow-on product. Wheeler bypassed the 3X because PS/2 development was at least a year ahead of 3X follow-on development, and developers were about to write the code for the PS/2.

Wheeler had to act quickly to convince the PS/2 developers to use the four-layer structure. He had to use all of his developed skills as well as some that lay dormant, including an ability to shake the trees of the IBM organization, to get the PS/2 developers to go along with him. It was imperative that he succeed.

In 1984, Akers and other MC members recognized that the PC market was growing faster than many other IBM markets and that PC technology was growing at a 20 to 25% compounded rate. When they looked ahead a few years, they saw a huge market that included a PC with 500 megabytes of storage. Because of the importance of the market and the impact that PC technology would have on all other types of computers, the MC decided it needed a good development strategy to assure IBM's leadership position in the PC market. The plan called for a PS/2 operating system that provided more functions than those of the original PC, which used PC-DOS or MS-DOS. The PS/2 could eventually interconnect smoothly with other IBM product families, and IBM could offer "seamless" cooperative, or enterprise-wide, processing solutions. Apparently Wheeler did not have to fell trees in a rain forest to get PS/2 developers to see the light. They agreed to adopt his structure.

At the end of 1984 or the beginning of 1985, the time was right to go after the developers of the 3X midrange products. To do this, Wheeler and his staff worked with Rochester. They pointed out that since the layered structure works for the OS/2 and all the 370s, it should also work for the midrange and the /38 operating system. The Rochester developers readily agreed that Wheeler's structure was the right one for the development of the 3X follow-on software and agreed to use the structure. Rochester recognized that if its product line were to be successful, it had to be an integral part of IBM's full product line.

This acceptance opened two avenues. First, although the public would not realize it for several years, IBM had completed the groundwork for linking its three armies of products and attacking the marketplace with the longest seamless product line the industry has ever seen. That had to happen before IBM could seriously think about offering distributed data and interconnected applications, let alone cooperative or enterprise solutions. It had to happen before IBM could think of offering software companies a market for their products that ran from the PS/2 through the 370 product line. Rochester's agreement provided the means for IBM's midrange developers, who often felt they were step children, to join the corporate family. It also laid the groundwork for bringing the /36 and /38, customers who often think of themselves as orphans, into the mainstream of IBM's product families.

Once the Rochester developers agreed to adopt the layered structure, Wheeler talked about software interfaces, such as SQL for relational data bases and the other interfaces that Taradalsky, Hanrahan, Casey, and Saranga had worked hard to establish across all the environments. Rochester quickly agreed that it should support common software interfaces.

Doubtless, Wheeler learned something from working with the midrange developers. He acquired a great appreciation of the problems that IBM's midrange organization faces in developing and selling /36s and /38s as stand-alone computers in medium-sized business establishments and as departmental computers in large enterprises. He had an opportunity to learn the world-class stature of the /38. Some aspects of the design were superior to the approach he and other 370 designers had taken.

1985—Vice President, Programming

In 1985, Wheeler advanced to Vice President of the Corporation. When Akers, Kuehler, and a few other executives agreed to move Wheeler into this prestigious position, the action signaled the rest of the executives near the top of the IBM hierarchy that Wheeler had the support of those at the very top.

Over the next year, Wheeler worked at refining the body of concepts that were the essence of his approach to structuring and redirecting the IBM software development effort. During this time, he also did something that many executives find difficult to do. He made sure that everyone who was helping to implement the structure took ownership of the project. Wheeler used many approaches to accomplish that. One approach was to bring a group of developers together and obtain agreement on what they would do next. Then he would invite them to accompany him to the Management Committee meeting. At the meeting, he would ask each of the developers to tell the MC what they planned to do. By stating their own plans, not Wheeler's plans, to the MC, they took a big step toward assuming ownership of the project. Wheeler used the same approach when the developers attained a major objective. He sent them over to the MC to report on their own accomplishments rather than doing it himself. This tactic emphasized the developers' ownership of the project. He used another technique to attain cooperation from team members—he donned the role of a coach. He constantly reminded the developers that this was their game, they were the real players, and all he could do was to play coach. If Shirley MacLaine's book *It's All in the Playing* had been in print at that time, Wheeler might have used the title to drive home his point. Another executive of equal technical ability would probably never have won the support Wheeler did, unless he too applied these approaches to motivating people.

A couple of IBM wild ducks have their opinions of why Wheeler was able to move people and mountains. One of Don Casey's assistants says, "All you have to do is observe the personal commitment that he (Wheeler) makes and you want to do the best you can." Ed Lassettre, IBM Fellow at the IBM Santa Teresa Lab, is very clear about Wheeler: "He's an extremely hard driving and dedicated person, but is not dogmatic."

Sometime in 1986, Akers, Kuehler, Krowe, and a few other top–level executives decided the time had come to take the structure that had developed and drive it across every aspect of the IBM Corporation and into the marketplace. Akers concluded that the structure was sound and sufficiently developed to enable him to attack a few problems. Too much atrophy had already set into the company; customers had begun to perceive that IBM had no grand strategy, and large investors began to think that all Akers could do to get the $50 billion plus giant to run as fast as it used to was to reduce the head count. Implementing the four-layer structure would hurl a preponderance of force at those problems.

But this raises a question about the wisdom of imposing this structure or any structure on the people of IBM.

The generally accepted notion is that to engage in original thought, make scientific discoveries, yield artistic originality, and produce great and unexpected accomplishments, an unstructured environment like that found in many of the high-tech, start-up companies is required. Most likely, these generally accepted notions are incorrect. With a good structure, the conscious and unconscious mind can see patterns and relationships that might otherwise be missed. For that reason, implementing the structure across the company, if it were to produce anything at all, might produce the spark that initiated a renaissance in IBM's thinking.

Shortly after Akers reached his decision, Wheeler called the four development executives together and told them the time had come for them, as layer managers,

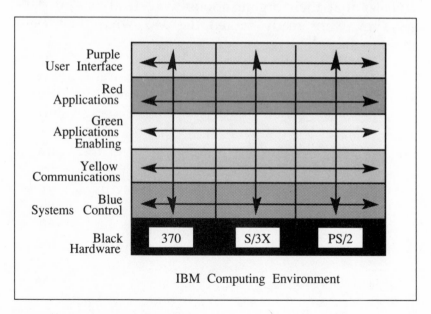

Figure 3 – The Structure of SAA

to extend their view. Taradalsky and Saranga must be concerned with not just the 370 but with the 3X and the PS/2 as well. Hanrahan was assigned to help develop the common user access across all three product lines. The result of their efforts across product lines would look like Figure 3. To obtain commitment from these key players, Wheeler called on all he had learned at Union College, the IBM Philadelphia branch office, the Air Force, Endicott, and the Kingston Lab. He also called upon his skills as systems designer, salesman, strategist, and coach to start the process of driving SAA across the entire company and the industry.

By noon on February 18, 1987, Wheeler was prepared to face the Management Committee. Four divisional development VPs and a marketing executive assured Wheeler that their organizations were ready to go public. They were ready to tell the MC what they were about to do.

22 Moment of Truth

A few minutes before 1:00 P.M., Peter Dance, accompanied by John Friedline, drove over to the Armonk parking lot. Ten minutes later, Earl Wheeler arrived with Morris Taradalsky seated next to him and Don Casey in the back seat. Dick Hanrahan and Mike Saranga drove their own vehicles.

At the reception desk, Dance and Friedline signed into the IBM Employee Guest Book, once called the Visitors Book. After the popular TV series *V* aired about "visitors"—creatures and reptiles from outer space that invaded Earth for "people food"—someone in IBM

231

thought it was distasteful for guests or IBM employees to be labeled "Visitors." Hence, the name of the guest register was changed to something less ghoulish.

Dance and Friedline walked directly to a door that separates the atrium from the rest of the building. The receptionist pressed a button, causing the door to open. Dance and Friedline took two quick steps through it, then turned sharply right. A short distance ahead, they abruptly turned right again and found themselves facing the elevator that would take them upstairs.

When the elevator doors opened, the men stepped in and Dance pressed the third floor button. In a couple of seconds the elevator, which could hold no more than five people comfortably, moved upward. After what seemed to be a long time, the elevator opened onto the third floor reception area. An attractive middle–aged woman greeted them from a desk. Dance stopped to tell her who they were.

Meanwhile, Friedline began looking about the room. As he wandered, he turned his head to his left and then suddenly stepped forward as if to dodge an on–coming person or object. Through the corner of his left eye, he glimpsed the outline of a man's face and shoulder. As he turned around, he laughed. There was John Opel, John Akers' predecessor, not walking toward him or standing next to the wall, but suspended on the wall. On the left wall, flush with the elevator door, an oil painting of Opel gazed out into the room at Friedline. The painting isn't noticed unless a guest takes a few steps into the reception area and turns around or looks backward. John laughed and said to himself, "Well, Opel still keeps me hopping."

Moments later he heard Dance say, "Hey John, there's

Learson, and Cary, and over there is Watson Senior. Watson Junior's over there—all IBM Chairmen."

"Hey, Pete, who is that woman over there in the white formal?" Of all the likenesses hanging on the walls, only one was a woman.

"I think that is Watson Senior's wife."

Then John asked, "Where's Akers?"

"I think you don't get hung here until you're a retired IBM Chairman," Peter replied.

The receptionist interrupted, saying, "That's not completely correct." She pointed to a blank space on the wall and explained that it was usually filled with a rotating exhibit of other works.

Dance, beginning to think about what he was going to say to the MC, distractedly murmured, "That's great, that's just great."

With that, Dance and Friedline took seats on the orange sectional chairs. Within minutes, a train of attendees began to flow by. Krowe, Kuehler, Akers, and Paul Rizzo walked in. Everyone nodded, smiled, or otherwise briefly acknowledged each of the others' presence. Akers recognized Dance, but not John Friedline. A few minutes later, the rest of the MC and some assistants filed in and briskly entered the MC conference room, closing the door behind them.

Just as the conference room door closed, the elevator doors on the opposite side of the reception area opened and someone within said, "You go first."

"No, after you."

Finally, saying "Okay, I'm getting out," Mike Saranga burst into the room. The other development executives trailed behind him.

"Hi, Pete. John."

Dance said, "Glad you all decided to come. I wouldn't want to do this alone."

"You needn't worry about that," Saranga replied.

Zero Hour Approaches

As the guests seated themselves, the reception room suddenly quieted. Some participants began to look over notes. Others stared distractedly at open magazines and newspapers while thinking about their presentations. Some just sat. No one admitted to stage jitters.

About 1:25 P.M., the conference room door opened. More than one of the presenters suddenly recalled the feeling they had had as children when the dentist's nurse walked into the reception area. But it was the AA who had worried so much about Crawford's speech, the Raleigh storm, and Don Casey's whereabouts who stepped into the reception area.

The AA walked over to Earl Wheeler, greeted him formally, and asked whether his party was ready.

"The name's Earl. Please call me Earl. Yes, we're ready."

"Great. Ah, can we just go over a few things to make sure everything goes smoothly?"

"Sure. Peter, Mike, won't you come over here, please?"

"First, how many of you will be going in?"

Earl replied, "Speaking just for the developers and myself, there will be five. Peter?"

Dance then said, "From the Field, I will be the only one." No reference was made to Friedline.

The AA said, "That makes six; okay."

Then the AA, Wheeler, and the other presenters worked out the logistics—who would speak first, where everyone would sit, and how long the presentations might take. As soon as everyone understood the game plan, the AA excused himself, quietly reopened the door to the conference room, and disappeared behind it. A minute or two later, a light flashed on the receptionist's phone. As soon as she put the receiver down, she glanced at Wheeler and said, "Mr. Wheeler, you and your party may go in now."

As Wheeler and the others walked toward the door, one of them nervously joked, "Wheeler party of six, your table's ready." Another warned, "Smile as you go by them [the MC members]—look like you're happy to see them." A third took a deep breath: "I'll be glad when this is over."

Hanrahan, Saranga, Taradalsky, Casey, and Dance, followed by Wheeler, entered the conference room at the right front corner. They felt like nervous college students walking into a lecture hall in front of the professor's podium as they filed in past the MC members. The four development executives and Peter Dance took seats in the second row and along the sides of the room. Earl Wheeler remained standing between the podium and the wall on the right.

The AA briefly introduced Wheeler, who then stepped to the podium. As Wheeler took charge of the lectern, he handed the AA a folder of transparencies. Within 20 minutes, Wheeler and everyone else in the room would regret that action.

The AA took the folder and walked across the room to the overhead projector. He was pleased that Wheeler had brought overheads—the MC prefers them. When 35-millimeter slides are used, the lights have to be dimmed, thus obscuring the very revealing facial expressions of the presenters.

Wheeler Speaks

Wheeler cleared his throat in the hushed room several times. He lowered his eyes to a second manila folder containing his notes. For a moment he thought, "What an insignificant, plain, simple cover. This unpretentious scrap of cardboard holds the contents of SAA—a powerful, immense architecture that holds the key to future computing, perhaps the key to IBM's future." SAA was like a crucible into which the lives, souls, will, and minds of these men had been poured. How unfitting and unjust a container for so important a task was this innocuous folder. How true of life. Returning from this stream of consciousness to the room, Wheeler lifted his eyes to meet those facing him.

"I'm pleased to see all of you again," he said, and he meant it. Akers and a few others in the front row nodded, smiled, or otherwise acknowledged him. This was about the eighth time in the last year that Wheeler had reported on the status of what eventually became SAA. Today was the most important of all the meetings.

Wheeler opened with an overview: "Today, I will briefly review why customers need SAA and some of the key benefits of SAA. I will also introduce the heads of the development team, who will each speak about their areas of technology and responsibility.

"I can categorically state that we can announce SAA on March 17 and that it is in our power to make SAA a reality in the marketplace within two years." As he said that, the AA placed the first transparency on the projector. It stated simply, *Systems Application Architecture.*

"I'll briefly set the stage to lead in to why customers need Systems Application Architecture." With that statement, he took a quick sip of water.

"To begin, the first computer systems available were hardware. Then, computer systems contained hardware, operating system, and applications software. Today, customers are talking about applications in an interconnected environment. That's what a computer system is today." Wheeler paused and said, "The essence of computing today is applications in an interconnected environment."

Everyone in the room knew exactly what Wheeler meant when he used the term *applications*—programs that are specific to the particular roles that a given computer performs within a given organization and that directly contribute to performing those roles. He also knew they understood what he meant by *interconnected* —multiple hardware and software systems distributed and connected throughout an enterprise. But Wheeler decided to elaborate.

"By interconnected applications, I mean applications that the user invokes that may say 'I need data,' and the system will be smart enough to say, 'Do I have the data, or is it somewhere else; if it's somewhere else, where is it throughout the multiple other systems? Bring back that data, join it, present it to the application.'

"What's important is that the user never need know that the system went a thousand miles away across many computer interconnections to get the data and present it to the application, which in turn presents it to the end user. The end user hasn't seen any effect, the application hasn't seen any effect, and the system has let the enterprise (the person who's managing the enterprise) decide where the data should be placed.

"Where an enterprise wants to place data today is not necessarily where they will want to place it tomorrow, so the enterprise should be able to build in that flexibility. The enterprise should decide where they want to do their network management and how they want to interconnect these things. Interconnected applications enable users to stop creating unique solutions that connect A to B but cannot connect C to B. Interconnected applications will eliminate that problem." Wheeler knew that he had rambled somewhat.

"This brings me to the integrated enterprise. We all know this is what the customers will want. Interconnected applications of course imply interconnected or distributed data bases. Our next major thrust will be the integrated enterprise system. And it's not a system that just takes copper or fiber optics and strings hardware together. We have to do it with software and do it in a way that's easy for us, easy for software companies, and easy for the ultimate customer.

"That means we have to offer customers a fully heterogeneous interconnect. You can truly interchange the operating systems as you form a very complex mesh network—a fully heterogeneous interconnect.

"But there's a lot we need to do to offer the customers integrated enterprise systems. A lot of problems need to be solved."

He paused, adjusted his notes, and then continued. "For a long time now, the scope and range of the IBM product line have demanded multiple hardware systems and multiple operating systems." They knew he meant the 370, 36, 38, and the PCs and their operating systems. At this point, one of the MC members interrupted to ask Wheeler to speak a little louder.

Slightly louder, he continued, "Each of these products has its own unique architecture. The individual performance of the various architectures that we have has been outstanding." He probably said that to disarm the members of the MC who had spent their professional careers helping to make the 370, 36, 38, or PC architectures a success.

At this point, Wheeler looked to his right and nodded to the AA, who placed on the overhead projector the transparency shown in Figure 1.

"We plan to interconnect four operating systems that support three hardware families." Pointing to the screen on his right he said, "We need to, in effect, interconnect the OS/2, the operating system of the follow-on

---

♦	OS/2, 3X Follow-on OS, MVS, and VM Operating Systems
♦	PS/2, 3X Follow-on, and 370 Hardware Environments

Figure 1 – The Scope of Systems Application Architecture

3X product, and the MVS and VM operating systems. If we do that, it will enable our customers to really start moving toward implementing integrated applications and integrated enterprise solutions."

At this point, Akers raised his hand and asked, "It will enable the customers to more quickly and easily cut through their applications backlog, won't it?" Akers knew the answer, of course. He may just have wanted to be sure that everyone in the room appreciated the pragmatic quality of what Wheeler was presenting.

For a moment Wheeler paused. Then he answered, "Sure, but we've got to do a lot of work to make that happen. But that brings me to the interfaces." Again, Wheeler turned his head to the right and nodded to the AA working the projector. The AA placed a slide that looked very much like Figure 2 on the projector.

Then Wheeler said, "We think that four different software interfaces hold the key to making it easier

```
Interfaces:

    ◆   Common User Access

    ◆   Common Applications

    ◆   Common Programming

    ◆   Common Communications Support

Scope:

    ◆   PS/2, 3X Follow–on, and
        370 Hardware Environments

    ◆   OS/2, 3X Follow–on OS, MVS,
        and VM
```

Figure 2 – Systems Application Architecture Interfaces

than ever for customers to cut their applications back-log down and to build interconnected applications and integrated enterprises. We need a common user, appli-cation, programming, and communication support interface across the four operating systems and three hardware environments. With those interfaces, users and programmers can leverage their knowledge and tools. These interfaces will be supported across OS/2, the 3X's operating system, and the two most important 370 operating systems, MVS and VM."

At this point, Allen Krowe interrupted. "You're leav-ing the RT PC (IBM's workstation product) out of this?"

"Yes, at this time. But we may be able to add it in later," said Wheeler.

"Fine, sorry to have interrupted you."

"Sure."

Someone else asked, "Mmm, how do you think the customers will take it when they hear we don't plan to include the original PC with its PC-DOS operating sys-tem and the 370 with the VSE operating system?"

"Well, I don't think it's going to be a problem. We may have to explain to the PC-DOS and VSE customer base that those two operating systems lack the functions needed to participate in an SAA environment. When they realize this, I don't think we'll have a problem."

"Besides," interjected Akers, "we want customers to buy new technology and products anyway."

Another MC member asked, "What about UNIX?"

"What about it?" Wheeler shot back. "If the cus-tomers demand UNIX, we can add it to the list of oper-ating systems that we support across the three hardware families. Technically it's certainly possible. It's a market-ing decision. It's a business decision."

Akers then added, "We have a task force studying what our UNIX business strategy should be. We can address that issue at a later date."

Wheeler continued, "This brings me to my second point—the benefits of Systems Application Architecture." He looked down at his notes and said, "Now, it's time to bring the 370, 3X, and PCs within a consistent framework to provide better productivity for customers and to improve ease of use. That is what Systems Application Architecture will do." He paused for a moment.

"Systems Application Architecture makes that new requirement of a computing system—interconnected applications—feasible." After he said that, he asked whether anyone had any questions. No one responded.

"We also believe we could do a better job of presenting those systems to the end users and to the people who write programs for them." When he said *systems* they again all knew that he meant the three hardware families and the four operating systems. Then he said, "Systems Application Architecture will provide a single, consistent presentation."

From the audience, someone again asked Wheeler to speak louder. Wheeler is very soft spoken—he must almost always be reminded to raise his voice when giving a speech. Today was no exception.

Wheeler again signaled for the next transparency, saying, "If applications functioning in an interconnected environment are what customers need, and I think they are, SAA provides the means to meet that challenge." Just as he said that, he heard the shishing sound of a half-dozen transparencies falling to the floor and a barely audible "God Dammit!"

Somehow, the AA had dropped the rest of Wheeler's slides. All eyes focused on the AA as he struggled to gather them up. They could not hear the AA saying, under his breath, "Dammit! That does it. They'll probably offer me Jackson Hole or Teheran as a sales territory after this screw up."

While the AA frantically collected the slides, Wheeler fielded a few questions. Then he signaled the AA for the next transparency. However, just as Wheeler started to say, "SAA provides . . .," he stopped. His words had no relationship to the words now projected on the screen.

"Ah, can you put up the transparency that has the SAA Benefits on it?" Wheeler requested.

Three seconds later, another group of words appeared on the screen and the AA said, "This is it, isn't it?"

Wheeler said, "No. It's the one that says *Benefits* at the top and ah, I believe, ah, it has *Cooperative Processing* and *Enterprise Processing* on it." The AA tried another. At this point, Wheeler apologized to the audience and quickly walked across the front of the room to help the AA find the right transparency.

After inspecting three or four overheads, he told the AA to forget it. He'd finish his presentation without the transparencies—he knew what he needed to say. At least at that moment in time, he thought he did.

As Wheeler slowly returned to the podium, he stopped at the center of the room and looked out at his audience. He started, "The real benefits of SAA are . . .," He paused. He began the same sentence again, and again paused. He apparently could not find the words to complete his thought.

Something was obviously wrong. Besides not being able to finish the sentence, he looked troubled and surprised.

As Wheeler continued to gaze straight ahead, his eyes focused on John Akers who sat in his line of sight.

Still staring straight ahead, Wheeler tried again, "The real benefits of SAA are . . .," and again, he stopped. The people in the room began looking along Wheeler's line of sight to see what absorbed his attention. From where Wheeler stood at the center of the room, he could see straight in front of him not only Akers, the present keeper of the great IBM company and its institutions, but also Thomas Watson Senior, the patriarch of the company.

Perhaps this powerful view of Akers and the portrait of Watson behind him made Wheeler reflect on a larger view of his proposal. What Wheeler was proposing was not just another plan to build a computer product—like The Eagle in Tracy Kidder's *The Soul of A New Machine*—this went way beyond that. Wheeler's proposal would alter the way millions of people would use computers and think about computing. It would also force hundreds of thousands of IBMers to change their thinking and method of operation. It would change the state of computing.

Momentarily, Wheeler, still staring straight at Akers and Watson said, "It's the view." What did he mean? Had that view of Akers with Watson majestically looming over him triggered something else deep in his mind? Did *view* have special meaning to Wheeler?

Wheeler searched to discover why the word *view* came to the forefront of his mind and his lips. Perhaps it was from the beliefs he had learned at Union College.

No, not "to gather and evaluate information," or "to think coherently," or "to form aesthetic judgments," but the one that states "to view a time and place from a perspective of knowledge." Ah, that's the phrase now circling in his head—to view a time and place from a perspective of knowledge. And it influenced what he was trying to say.

Wheeler groped—trying to clarify the perception that it takes great knowledge of computer users, programmers, system analysts, software companies, IBM employees, and others to envision the problems in time and place that they faced, using computers. Mentally, he viewed the multiplicity of people and the problems each of them faced and he tried to formulate a simple and all-inclusive statement for what SAA would do for all of them.

The word *common* kept resurfacing, too. Perhaps it was because it permeated so many discussions and elements of SAA—a common user interface, common programming environment, common communications.

View—Common. Common—View. Common View.

Was this what he was looking for? Were these the words that hit the mark? Was this the essence of Systems Application Architecture—a common view?

It must have all come together, because Wheeler suddenly said, "The benefit of Systems Application Architecture is that it creates a Common View. No, not a singular Common View for everyone, but a different Common View, depending on who you are and what your perspective is. Looking from each perspective, there's a common view."

With more confidence he continued, "SAA provides" (he paused briefly to do some quick arithmetic) "six or perhaps seven different types of people with a Common View."

Dance, Morris, the other VPs, and all the members of the MC listened closely. Something had inspired Earl Wheeler.

"SAA enables users of our future line of PCs and midrange products, and of the 370 system, to see a common view. The common user interface makes that possible.

"SAA enables programmers to have a common view of the tools and services across the four operating environments. The common programming interface makes that possible."

"SAA enables systems analysts planning multisystem implementations to see a common view of communication services across the four operating environments."

In the back of the room, Dance leaned over to Dick Hanrahan and whispered, "I like the sound of it."

When Wheeler paused for a moment, Jack Kuehler said, "And I can see how SAA will give all our employees a common view. It gives them a new focus. They know where to concentrate their resources."

Krowe said, "I can see how SAA can give our competitors one hell of a Common View." With that the room filled with laughter. Krowe continued, "It gives them the broadest line of, in a way, homogeneous products to compete against."

Paul Rizzo, said, "Yeah, it's like the days when we had a single family of 360s. One common view of that product."

Earl Wheeler took the floor again. "SAA will provide

a spectrum of common views depending on who you are and how and where you look.

Wheeler walked back to the podium. The AA followed and handed him the transparency. Wheeler smiled a bit and told the AA it was okay. To himself he thought that had there not been a slip up, he might never have stumbled onto these insights.

After that dynamic experience, there wasn't much more for Wheeler to say. He finished by passing the podium on, stating that the development executives and the marketing representative, to whom they all owed a big debt of thanks for the tremendous job they had done on this project, would each speak on the status of his own area of responsibility in regard to SAA. A vote of thanks was also due the committee, Wheeler said, especially Messrs. Krowe, Akers, and Kuehler, for its support of this project. He then retired to the back of the room, and the AA introduced, one after another, the four development VPs and Peter Dance.

Each of the VPs spoke for no more than 15 minutes. Mike Saranga told a joke to lighten up his topic, Morris Taradalsky demonstrated his deep understanding of all the technical challenges, Hanrahan demonstrated the depth of his control of every aspect of his project, and Casey self–assuredly presented communications support. They were all ready to launch SAA. Peter Dance told the committee that the field and the team players were ready to kick off SAA on March 17.

After putting a few questions to team members, John Akers and members of the MC seemed satisfied. Akers nodded to Wheeler and thanked them all for their excellent work. With that, the Wheeler party left the

MC meeting as they had come—through the door at the right front of the room.

The receptionist watched the six presenters and Friedline congratulate each other in the reception area. Wheeler made a point to tell each of them in a different way that the team could not have accomplished what it did without their specific contributions. But they, too, knew how important Wheeler's role was and would continue to be. Without him, this project might never have happened.

It never dawned on them that the MC had not really given a formal okay; at least no precise words had been spoken. But then, they hadn't gone to that meeting for a yea or nay. They went because they knew they had everything worked out.

Amid the handshaking and back clapping, Dance and Friedline extricated themselves and prepared to head for the parking lot. They told Wheeler they wanted to rush over to Ryebrook (headquarters of the field sales and marketing division) to break the news to Larry Ford and his boss, Ed Lucente, who headed the field organization. The field had no more than a month to prepare for the Saint Patrick's Day announcement. Dance wanted to get the troops moving right away. Wheeler certainly understood.

The rest of them—Mike Saranga, Dick Hanrahan, Morris Taradalsky, Don Casey, and Earl Wheeler—began to unwind. Eventually, they too walked to their cars. But as they drove down Old Orchard Road past the apple trees on the right and the guard station on the left, they all could feel the high of participating in a major event. Today marked the end of one phase of this project and one intense period in their lives. It foretold the beginning of an even more monumental one—implementation of the Systems Application Architecture strategy.

Later in the day as the sky darkened, Jack Kuehler, Allen Krowe, Paul Rizzo, and other members of the MC headed home. Wheeler's SAA strategy, to them, held the promise of revitalizing IBM, its people, and its marketplace. It could be the spark that would set off a renaissance in this somewhat lethargic, but still great computer company.

Akers, the former Navy pilot from Oakland, California was the last to leave. He was thoughtful as he headed down Old Orchard Road. Any of a hundred thoughts could have been running through his mind: "It's decisive. . . It concentrates our resources. . . We have to make it happen fast." He may also have thought that the sooner customers, IBM employees, and the software companies would see the Common View, the happier he would be.

One of the next things he would have to do would be to bring the 3X follow-on—Silverlake—to the market.

Appendix:
IBM Programming
Announcement

MARCH 17, 1987

IBM Systems Application Architecture

Today, IBM announces IBM Systems Application Architecture, a collection of selected software interfaces, conventions and protocols that will be published in 1987.

IBM Systems Application Architecture will be the framework for development of consistent applications across the future offerings of the major IBM computing environments—System/370, System/3X, and Personal Computer.

251

Highlights

Systems Application Architecture provides the foundation for IBM to enhance the consistency of IBM software products by:

- Providing a common programming interface,
- Providing common communications support,
- Providing a common user access,
- Offering common applications,
- Enhancing the availability and consistency of National Language implementation.

Description

IBM offers systems based on several different hardware architectures and system control programs. By pursuing a multiple-architecture strategy, IBM has been able to provide products with outstanding price/performance to meet our customers' requirements. Today, IBM's products support the information processing needs of people in very different environments.

IBM Systems Application Architecture makes it easier for IBM's broad product line to solve customer information processing needs by providing the framework for the development and delivery of IBM products that address consistency requirements across the major IBM systems. Systems Application Architecture provides the foundation for IBM

- To enhance the consistency of IBM software products;
- To define a common programming interface with which customers, independent software vendors and IBM can productively develop applications that can be integrated with each other and ported to

run in multiple IBM Systems Application Architecture environments;

- To define common communications support that
  will provide interconnection of systems and programs and cross-system data access;
- To define a common user access, including screen
  layout, menu presentation and selection techniques, keyboard layout and use, and display
  options;
- To offer common IBM applications that run in
  each of the major computing environments.

Delivery of the IBM Systems Application Architecture will be evolutionary, beginning this year and continuing on an ongoing basis. This is the beginning of a
long-term strategy similar to the process that has implemented IBM Systems Network Architecture (SNA).
SNA started as a framework for consistency in the communications environment and has continued to be
enhanced and extended. Today, SNA is the basis of communications for IBM's products and for many other
vendors' products. In addition, IBM will continue to
invest in applications and systems software that is specific to particular computing environments.

Elements of the Architecture

IBM Systems Application Architecture consists of four
related elements—two of which are new (Common
User Access and Common Programming Interface).
The third is based on extensions to today's existing com-
munications architectures (Common Communications
Support). These three establish the basis for the fourth,
Common Applications, developed by IBM to be consis-

tent across systems. Independent software vendors and customers developing applications for IBM's major systems will also be encouraged to use IBM Systems Application Architecture products.

In addition, Systems Application Architecture provides IBM with the foundation to enhance the availability and consistency of National Language implementation in software products.

Common User Access: The Common User Access defines the basic elements of the end user interface and how to use them. The primary goal is to achieve (through consistency of user interface) transfer of learning, ease of learning, and ease of use across the range of IBM Systems Application Architecture applications and environments.

The Common User Access is a definition for IBM-developed software to adhere to over time and will be published so that customers and independent software vendors can develop programs that follow this definition.

Common Programming Interface: The Common Programming Interface is the application programming interface to the Systems Application Architecture systems. This interface consists of the languages and services used to develop productively applications that can be integrated with other applications and ported to run in multiple IBM Systems Application Architecture environments.

IBM is defining a Common Programming Interface that enables an application to be developed using IBM Systems Application Architecture products in one environment and then ported to another Systems Application Architecture environment with minimal changes to the application. This can result in increased programmer productivity and wider applicability of applications.

The initial elements of the Common Programming Interface are

- COBOL
  Based on ANS (American National Standard) Programming Language COBOL, X3.23—1985 Intermediate Level.

- FORTRAN
  Based on ANS Programming Language FORTRAN, 77 level.

- C
  Based on the draft proposed ANS Standard (X3J11).

- Application Generator
  Based on elements of the interfaces found in the existing Cross System product.

- Procedures Language
  Based on the existing REXX language.

- Database Interface
  Based on the ANS Database Language SQL, X3.135 —1986, and IBM's SQL (Structured Query Language).

- Query Interface
  Based on an extension of the interfaces found in today's Query Management Facility (QMF) product.

- Presentation Interface
  Based on extensions to the interface found in key elements of today's Graphical Data Display Manager (GDDM) product, provides services to present textual and graphic information on displays, printers and plotters.

- Dialog Interface
  Based on extensions to the interface found in
  today's EZ-VU product, provides for the definition,
  display, and management of textual information
  and menus, and for the control of screen flow within applications.

This Common Programming Interface provides a
basis for customers and independent software vendors
to use IBM Systems Application Architecture products
to develop portable applications. Additional elements
will be defined and the elements named above will be
extended. The long range goal is to define a comprehen-
sive and productive set of IBM programming development languages and services.

Common Communications Support: Common Communications Support is used to interconnect Systems
Application Architecture applications, Systems Application Architecture systems, communication networks
and devices. This will be achieved by the consistent
implementation of designated communication architectures in each of the Systems Application Architecture
environments. The architectures announced here are
the building blocks for distributed function to be de-
tailed in future announcements of Common Programming Interfaces and IBM Systems Application Architecture applications.

The architectures selected have been chosen largely
from Systems Network Architecture (SNA) and international standards. Each was also included in the Open
Communications Architectures announcement of September 16, 1986 (Programming Announcement 286-
410), thus reaffirming IBM's commitment to openness.

As IBM expands the Systems Application Architecture, additional communications architectures will be evaluated for inclusion in Common Communications Support.

Included in Common Communications Support at this time are:

Data Streams:

- 3270 Data Stream
  The 3270 Data Stream consists of user-provided data and commands, as well as control information that governs the way data is handled and formatted by IBM displays and printers. The Systems Application Architecture computing environments will all support the 3270 Data Stream. In addition, the System/3X family will continue to support the 5250 Data Stream. The 3270 Data Stream is documented in the *IBM 3270 Information Display System Data Stream Programmer's Reference* (GA23-0059).

- Document Content Architecture
  Document Content Architecture defines the rules for specifying the form and meaning of a text document. It provides for uniform interchange of textual information in the office environment and consists of format elements optimized for document revision. This is documented in *Document Content Architecture: Revisable-Form-Text Reference* (SC23-0758).

- Intelligent Printer Data Stream (IPDS)
  IPDS is the high function data stream intended for use with all points addressable page printers.

Planned availability for documentation of this data stream is third quarter of 1987.

Application Services:

- SNA Distribution Services (SNADS)
  SNADS provides an asynchronous distribution capability in an SNA network, thereby avoiding the need for active sessions between the end points. SNADS is documented in *Systems Network Architecture Format and Protocol Reference Manual: Distribution Services* (SC30-3098).

- Document Interchange Architecture (DIA)
  DIA provides a set of protocols that define several common office functions performed cooperatively by IBM products. This is documented in *Document Interchange Architecture: Technical Reference* (SC23-0781).

- SNA Network Management Architecture
  SNA Network Management Architecture describes IBM's approach to managing communication networks. The protocols of problem management offer a vehicle for monitoring network operations from a central location. This is documented in *Format and Protocol Reference Manual: Management Services* (SC30-3346).

Session Services:

- LU Type 6.2
  LU Type 6.2 is a program-to-program communication protocol. It defines a rich set of interprogram communication services including a base subset and optional supplementary services. Support of

the base is included in IBM LU6.2 products that expose an LU6.2 application programming interface. This ensures compatibility of communication functions across systems. LU6.2 is documented in *Systems Network Architecture: Format and Protocol Reference Manual, Architecture Logic for LU Type 6.2* (SC30-3269).

Network:

- Low-Entry Networking Node
  A SNA *Low-Entry Networking Node* (Type 2.1 node) supports peer-to-peer communication. Type 2.1 nodes can be either programmable or fixed function systems. SNA Low-Entry Networking allows, through a common set of protocols, multiple and parallel SNA sessions to be established between Type 2.1 nodes that are directly attached to each other. Low-Entry Networking is documented in *Systems Network Architecture Format and Protocol Reference Manual: Architecture Logic for Type 2.1 Nodes* (SC30-3422).

- X.25
  X.25 defines a packet-mode interface for attaching data terminal equipment (DTE) such as host computers, communication controllers, and terminals to packet-switched data networks. An IBM-defined external specification, *The X.25 Interface for Attaching SNA Nodes to Packet-Switched Data Networks General Information Manual* (GA27-3345) and the 1984 version of this interface (GA27-3761) describe the elements of CCITT X.25 that are applicable to IBM SNA products that can attach to X.25 networks.

Data Link Controls:

- Synchronous Data Link Control (SDLC)
  SDLC is a discipline for managing synchronous, code-transparent, serial-by-bit information transfer between nodes that are joined by telecommunication links. This is documented in *IBM Synchronous Data Link Control Concepts* (GA27-3093).

- IBM Token-Ring Network
  The *IBM Token-Ring Network* consists of a wiring system (the IBM Cabling System), a set of communication adapters (stations) and an access protocol that controls the sharing of the physical medium by the stations attached to the LAN. The IBM Token-Ring Architecture is based on the IEEE 802.2 and 802.5 standards. This is documented in *Token-Ring Network Architecture Reference* (part number 6165877).

Common Applications: It is IBM's intent to develop common applications across the Systems Application Architecture environments. The initial focus is on office applications and, later, industry-specific applications. With the publications that define the IBM Systems Application Architecture and the availability of products, IBM is encouraging independent software vendors and customers to develop applications based on IBM Systems Application Architecture products.

As with the Common Programming Interface, elements are being defined for office applications. The elements being defined include:
- Document Creation,
- Document Library,

- Personal Services, Mail,
- Decision Support.

Summary

IBM Systems Application Architecture is a set of software interfaces, conventions and protocols—a framework for productively designing and developing applications with cross-system consistency. Systems Application Architecture defines the foundation to build portable, consistent application systems for the future with IBM hardware, control programs, and IBM Systems Application Architecture products.

Publications

The following publications are the primary deliverables planned for the Systems Application Architecture in 1987:

- *Systems Application Architecture Overview* (GC26-4341)
  This publication introduces Systems Application Architecture concepts and provides the initial designation of the systems and products participating in Systems Application Architecture. Planned availability is second quarter of 1987.
- Common User Access Publication
  A reference manual is planned to be available in the third quarter of 1987. It will specify the common user access interfaces for intelligent workstations. Specifications for common user access interfaces for main-frame interactive terminals is planned to be added to this specification in the

fourth quarter of 1987. The elements to be specified include screen layout, menu presentation and selection techniques, keyboard layout and use, and display options.

- Common Programming Interface Publications
Reference manuals are planned to describe each interface that participates in application enabling for Systems Application Architecture. These reference manuals will provide the grammar and syntax (supplemented by the programming guidance provided by the products that implement the interface) needed to develop applications for the Systems Application Architecture environments. The publications and their planned availability dates follow:

Title	Available
Common Programming Interface COBOL Reference	3Q87
Common Programming Interface FORTRAN Reference	3Q87
Common Programming Interface C Reference	3Q87
Common Programming Interface Procedures Language Reference	3Q87
Common Programming Interface Application Generator Reference	3Q87
Common Programming Interface Query Reference	3Q87

Common Programming Interface
Database Reference   3Q87

Common Programming Interface
Presentation Reference   3Q87

Common Programming Interface
Dialog Reference   3Q87

- Writing Portable Programs
  This publication provides guidance on developing application programs that are consistent and portable among Systems Application Architecture systems. These applications will use the common Programming Interfaces and implement the Systems Application Architecture Common User Access specification. Planned availability is third quarter of 1987.

- Common Communications Support Publications
  The section Common Communications Support names the publications that define Systems Application Architecture communications protocols and standards.

Glossary

AA. Administrative Assistant.

ADAPSO. Formerly The Association of Data Processing Services Organization, now called The Computer Software and Services Industry Association.

AI. Artificial Intelligence.

AIX. Advanced Interactive Executive operating system.

ANS. American National Standard.

APL. A Programming Language.

ATM. Automated Teller Machine.

AT&T. American Telephone & Telegraph.

Application. The use to which an information processing system is put, e.g., payroll, airline reservation network applications.

Architecture. The organizational structure of a computer system including software and hardware.

Batch. Accumulation of data to be processed.

Bit. Binary Digit.

Byte. Equal to eight bits.

C. A programming language.

CADAM. Computer-Graphics Augmented Design and Manufacturing.

CCITT. International Telegraph and Telephone Consultative Committee. International forum for establishing telecommunications system standards; comprises representatives from government-run and privately owned networks and major network equipment suppliers.

CCS. Common Communication Support.

CDC. Control Data Corporation.

COBOL. Common Business Oriented Language, a programming language.

Communication. (See Data Communication.)

COPICS. Communications Oriented Production and Information Control System.

CPD. Communications Product Division.

CPI. Common Programming Interface.

CSP. Cross Systems Product.

CUA. Common User Access.

DASD. Direct Access Storage Device.

Data Base. A collection of data fundamental to a system or enterprise.

Data Communication. The transfer of information between functional units by means of data transmission according to a protocol.

Data Link. The interconnecting data circuit and the link protocol between two or more pieces of equipment.

Data Processing (DP). Systematic performance of oper-

ations on data, e.g., handling, merging, sorting, computing.

Data Stream. All data transmitted through a data chan-
nel in a single read or write operation.

DB2. Data Base Two.

DBM. Data Base Management System.

DCA. Document Content Architecture.

DEC. Digital Equipment Corporation.

DIA. Document Interchange Architecture.

Distributed Data Processing. The distribution of processing function and data throughout an organization
to the locations where they are needed. The elements of
distributed processing may include a central processing
complex, distributed small systems, and programmable
workstations for remote processing, a communications
network with the ability to link the central and remote
sites, and a network control system to manage the flow
of information.

DL/1. Data Language/One. A data base management
system.

DOS. Disk Operating System.

DPCX. Distributed Processing Control Executive.

DPPX. Distributed Processing Programming Executive

ESD. Entry Systems Division.

Extended Addressing. A direct-addressing mode that
can access any area in storage.

FAA. Federal Aviation Agency.

Fiber Optics. Thin transparent fibers of glass or plastic
that are enclosed by material of a lower index of refrac-
tion and that transmit light throughout their length by
internal reflections. Use of fiber optics technology.

FORTRAN.   Formula Translation, a programming language.

Front-end Processor.   In a computer network, relieves a host computer of processing tasks sent as line control, message handling, code conversion, and error control.

GDDM. Graphical Data Display Manager.

GE. General Electric Company.

GEISCO. General Electric Information Services Company.

Gigabit. A unit of information equal to one billion bits.

GIS. General Information System.

Hardware. The parts of a computer you can touch.

Host.   In a computer network, a computer that provides end users with services such as computations and data bases and that performs network control functions.

HP. Hewlett-Packard Company.

ICL. International Computers, Inc.

IIS. IBM Information Services.

IMS. Information Management System.

Information Display.   A display that presents information such as the status of the system to a user but rarely requests a response.

Interactive.   Pertaining to a program or system that alternately accepts input and then responds.

Interface. A shared boundary; may be a hardware component to link two devices or a portion of storage or registers accessed by two or more computer programs.

LAN. Local Area Network.

Language. A set of characters, conventions, and rules that is used for conveying information.

LEN. Low-Entry Networking Node.

LISP. LISt Processing.

LU6.2. Logical Unit 6.2. Provides peer-to-peer communications between small-system nodes and S/370 hosts or other small systems via SNA backbone networks.

Mainframe. A large computer, particularly one to which other computers can be connected so they can share facilities provided by the mainframe .

MAP. Manufacturing Automation Protocol.

MAPICS. Manufacturing Accounting Production Information and Control System.

MC. IBM's Management Committee.

Memory. Main storage where instructions are executed.

MIPS. Millions of Instructions Per Second.

MIS. Management Information System.

MIT. Massachusetts Institute of Technology.

MVS. Multiple Virtual Storage.

MVS/XA. Multiple Virtual Storage/Extended Architecture.

Network. A configuration of data processing devices and software connected for information interchange.

NCP. Network Control Program.

OEM. Original Equipment Manufacturer.

Operating System (OS). Software that controls the execution of programs.

OSI. Open Systems Interconnection.

PBX. Private Branch Exchange.

PC AT. Personal Computer AT. IBM personal computer that runs many programs written for other IBM PCs as much as three times faster.

PC-DOS. An IBM disk operating system based on Microsoft Corporation's MS-DOS that operates with all

IBM personal computers.

PL/1. Programming Language One. A language designed for numeric scientific computations, business data processing, systems programming, and other applications.

Processor. The functional unit that interprets and executes instructions.

PROFS. Professional Office System.

Program. A sequence of instructions suitable for processing by a computer.

PROLOG. A non-procedural language.

Protocol. A set of semantic and syntactical rules that determines the behavior of functional units in achieving communications.

Prototyping. Developing a model suitable for evaluating a system, design, performance, and production potential.

PS/2. Personal System Two.

QMF. Query Management Facility.

R&D. Research and Development.

Relational Data Base. A data base organized and accessed according to relationships between data items.

REXX. A procedural language.

ROTC. Reserve Officers' Training Corps.

RPG. Report Program Generator.

RT PC. A microprocessor-based workstation system used for the computing needs of CAD/CAM, engineering and scientific, academic, and other professional environments.

SAA. Systems Application Architecture.

SDLC. Synchronous Data Link Control.

Session. The period of time during which a user of a terminal can communicate with an interactive system; usually elapsed time between logon and logoff.

SNA. System Network Architecture. IBM's hierarchical, layered network architecture for interconnected systems, hardware, and software. SNA networks comprise multiple nodes—nodes are embodied in mainframe computers, front-end processors, remote processors, and terminals.

SNADS. System Network Architecture Distributed Services.

Software. Programs, procedures, rules, and any associated documentation pertaining to the operation of a system.

SQL. Structured Query Language.

STL. Santa Teresa Labs.

System/36, System/38. General-purpose data processing systems for interactive and batch processing.

System/360. Large mainframe computing system to which other computers can be connected to share facilities.

System/370. Large mainframe computing system to which other computers can be connected to share facilities.

Time Share. To use a device for two or more interleaved purposes.

Time Sharing. A method of using a competing system that allows a number of users to execute programs concurrently and to interact with the programs during execution.

Telecommunication. Transmission of data between computer systems over telecommunication lines and between a computer system and remote devices.

Terminal. A device, usually having a keyboard and display screen for sending and receiving information.

Token-Ring Network. A ring network that allows unidirectional data transmission between data stations by a token passing procedure over one transmission medium so the transmitted data returns to the transmitting station.

Topology. Topology is considered a part of network architecture. There are three generic forms of topology: star, ring, and bus.

TSS. Time Sharing System. A programming system that provides users with conversational on-line access to a computing system with one or more processing units and simultaneously processes batched jobs.

UNIX. A trademark of the operating system introduced by Bell Laboratories in 1971 for DEC PDP minicomputers.

Virtual Disk. In VM, all or a logical subdivision of a physical disk storage device that has its own address, consecutive space for data, and an index or description of stored data so that the data can be accessed.

Virtual Printer. In VM, a printer simulated on disk by the control program for a virtual machine.

VM. Virtual Machine.

VSE. Virtual Storage Extended.

VTAM. Virtual Telecommunications Access Method. Together with the Network Control Program, a host-located VTAM provides the SNA transport layer (transport network) and many of the control and service functions needed by SNA backbone networks. VTAM provides application program access to NCP-managed sessions with terminals, remote applications, small systems applications or remote hosts.

Workstation. A configuration of input and output equipment at which an operator works.

3X. Family of general purpose midrange data processing computers.

5GL. Fifth Generation Language.

Trademarks

Frame Maker™ is a trademark of Frame Technology Corporation. WordStar™ is a trademark of MicroPro International Corporation. PageMaker® is a registered trademark of Aldus Corporation. dBASE III® is a registered trademark of Ashton–Tate Corporation. Word is trademarked in conjunction with Microsoft Corporation: Microsoft® Word. Ventura Publisher is trademarked in conjunction with Xerox Corporation: Xerox® Ventura Publisher. SuperCalc®3 is a registered trademark of Computer Associates International, Inc. Lotus 1–2–3® is a registered trademark of Lotus Development Corporation.

Index

DATE DUE

MAR 2 2 1989			